Spirit AWAKENING

Katherine —

As you open your
Spirit you will open
the spirit of others. —
And then Healing
will occur!
All the best!
Elaine

WaKan Tanka
Great Mystery,
teach me how to trust
my heart,
my mind,
my intuition,
my inner knowing,
the senses of my body,
the blessings of my Spirit.
Teach me to trust these things
so that I may enter my Sacred Space
and Love beyond my fear,
and thus Walk in Balance
with the passing of each
glorious Sun.

Lakota Prayer

ELAINE M. GROHMAN
IS ALSO THE AUTHOR OF

THE ANGELS AND ME
EXPERIENCES OF RECEIVING AND SHARING
DIVINE COMMUNICATIONS

HER EVENTS AND WORKSHOP SCHEDULE
IS AVAILABLE ON HER WEBSITE:

WWW.ELAINEGROHMAN.COM

LISTEN TO ARCHIVED INTERVIEWS ON HER WEBSITE.

LOOK FOR HER THIRD BOOK
DUE FOR RELEASE IN 2012
PUBLISHED BY INLIGHT, LLC

INLIGHT, LLC

DEDICATION

*This book is dedicated
to all people of Mother Earth,
and to those individuals who work to bring
about a lasting and meaningful Peace.*

One by one we evolve through Time.

*Each Life is a Blessing.
Each Life will experience Challenge.
Each Life can initiate Peace.*

*We need one another. We need ourselves.
And we need our Precious Earth
to survive and flourish.*

*It is my hope that these
Spirit Messages,
and the stories that accompany them,
will touch your heart,
and open your mind
as they have done for me.*

*I thank my parents,
the late Jack and Elaine Hughes,
for their courage in bringing all of their
children into the World.*

The author of this book does not dispense medical advice or prescribe the use of any technique as a form of treatment for physical, emotional or medical problems. One should seek the advice of his/her physician or healthcare provider. The intent of the author is to offer information of a general nature to help the reader in his/her quest for self-awareness and well-being. In the event that you use any of the information provided in this book for yourself, which is your right, the author and/or the publisher assume no responsibility for your actions.

Library of Congress Control Number: 2011919846
Grohman, Elaine M.

ISBN # 978-0-615-52275-3
Printed in the United States of America

Publisher's Cataloging-in-Publication Data
Grohman, Elaine M.
Spirit awakening : wisdom for life and living / Elaine M. Grohman. --
Farmington Hills, Mich. : InLight, c2011.
p. ; cm.
ISBN: 978-0-615-52275-3
Summary: Let your spirit awaken to the potential within you.
1. Energy medicine. 2. Self-care, Health. 3. Angels.
4. Spirituality. 5. Spiritual healing. 6. Intuition. I. Title.

RZ421 .G76 2011   2011919846
615.8528--dc23   1112

INLIGHT, LLC

WISDOM FOR LIFE
AND LIVING

ELAINE M. GROHMAN

INLIGHT, LLC

TABLE OF CONTENTS

TABLE OF CONTENTS

ELAINE M. GROHMAN

INTRODUCTION

"If we have no peace,
it is because we have forgotten
that we belong to each other."
Mother Teresa

I listen beyond words, I hear beyond sounds and I see with a vision that allows me to comprehend farther than what is presently before me. I do this every day, and you do too. My name is Elaine Grohman and I am an Energy Healer. My hands emit a beautiful quality of comfort and energy that can help to soothe the wounds that others carry. Your hands do too. I am an Angel Reader, an intuitive voyager and my ears hear beyond the spoken word as I listen to Life's Melody – a melody that guides us, embraces us, comforts us and encourages us to live our Lives fully in the knowledge that Love is what we are seeking. You are on the same voyage.

Spirit Awakening is just that - an opportunity for our Spirits to Awaken from our slumber, our collective nightmare, to work together to bring about the Dream that Life promises. We all dream of a happy, productive, love-filled life but perhaps we have neglected to make the necessary changes to bring that dream to fruition. First, we must look within ourselves in order to choose to ignite the Flame of Love that is in every cell of our bodies. With honesty and compassion we should take the time to pause and witness the thoughts we think, the feelings we emote and the decisions that spawn our actions, asking one crucial question, "Is

Love at work within me?" If the answer is "yes," bless you, and keep going. More often, the answer may be a reluctant "no." The "no" to Love is a block to Spirit and to a more peaceful, joyful Life.

Far too often we have held tightly to our wounds, our angers and our opinions. You can do that if you choose, but it is inevitable that poison held will poison the one who holds it. We see this every day. Stress is the number one precursor to illness, and stress is reflective of how we respond to life's circumstances.

I am a witness of Life - a momentary visitor in the lives of others. In the time that I spend with people it is my hope to open a door to change, perhaps giving someone the space to look differently at their Life so that they can begin to live more fully.

Spirit Awakening is a gift given to me that I am grateful to be able to share with you. My first book, The Angels and Me – Experiences of Receiving and Sharing Divine Communication, started me on this journey of sharing my life as an Energy Healer and Angel Reader. In this book, I have chosen to use the term "Spirit" rather than "Angel" in order to be more inclusive of the countless ways in which we interact with the Unseen. This also serves to illustrate how my perception has broadened from my initial language and understanding.

Angels have been a comfort to me since childhood and gave me a means of conceptualizing something beyond myself. My awareness continues to expand. The Spirit of Creation is in all that surrounds us, all that embraces us, all that challenges us and all that we are. We are in Spirit and Spirit is within us: there is no separation, except within our own limited thinking. "Spirit" has no religious distinction and is a universal reference to Creation. This is not to dismiss the content of "The Angels and Me," but serves to illustrate my broadening perspective as my thinking has expanded to be inclusive of all concepts of our interconnectedness. Knowingly or unknowingly, all people of Mother Earth interact with Spirit.

Each chapter begins with a Spirit Message, intuitive insights shared with me as I prepared to do group readings. These messages are typed in italics. Each and every time the communication seemed to be crafted to suit the audience, honing in on problems within the Human Heart that needed attention. Following the Spirit Message are my thoughts and experiences that illustrate its connection to every day life.

Spirit guides us towards change. Change does not have to be painful; in fact it can bring about great Peace, often in an instant, when we give ourselves permission to look at things differently. When we cease reacting to foolishness, we stop the foolishness from continuing. It's a good feeling to lay down your need to defend and allow Love to be the Agent of Change.

Life is our most precious Gift. It would serve us well to remember that Truth. Every day we are surrounded by opportunities to open our Hearts to the Love that could heal this Planet, our Home, Mother Earth, and in the process, we could heal ourselves.

Spirit has always been with us - guiding us, teaching us, providing for us and keeping us from harm. Spirit is in all things. The Earth that we walk upon and the stars in the sky are expressions of the Love that is Spirit in Action… Creation in Action… Life in Action.

We can no longer separate ourselves from the reality of our

choices. Collectively, humanity has not always done a good job. Individually, neither have we. But all of that can change, if we choose to listen to the wise counsel of Spirit and act upon that counsel with open and Loving Hearts. If we do not, it may be too late for us all.

We are being given the opportunity to look differently at our lives and the way that we live them. We all could improve; there is little doubt of that. The guidance of our Divine Companions never ceases to nudge us toward goodness… the kind of goodness that begins as a spark of recognition that things can change, starting with each and every thought we engage, each and every action we take, each and every word we speak. We must begin with ourselves.

We must be willing to know this certain Truth. We share this Precious Planet, our Mother Earth. This is our Home. All of Her resources, all of Her gifts and all of Her beauty are here for all of us, not a select few. If you have been born, there is a purpose for your Life. It is the Journey of your Lifetime to discover that purpose.

We can no longer afford to be blinded by our ignorance, pretending that we don't know better, for we certainly do. All that we hold dear is struggling to survive our ambivalence and is pleading with us to change. Our families, our institutions, our governance… all need to clean up their acts and begin to act as a member of a Healthy Family.

Yet, before we admonish ourselves, take Heart. Thousands upon thousands of people are beginning to see the Light – literally and figuratively. That Light is Love. Love is and will forever be the Balm that heals our self-imposed wounds. But before those wounds can heal, we have to acknowledge what has caused them in the first place. We have.

All of Humanity...every Woman, Man and Child has a right to be here. Each Life is no less Sacred than our own. There are simple steps that we must take to bring about a change, and each and every one of us is capable of initiating that change.

It begins with a Change of Heart. It begins with Making Different Choices – choices that are life sustaining, not life threatening.

Together we can create a chain reaction of goodness, allowing it to spread across the land, touching every heart, every part of Nature and every memory that supports that growth.

Spirit is known by many names: Angels, Guides, Honorable Ancestors and the like. It matters not what you call them - what matters is that you listen. Throughout the book you will notice words capitalized that may not normally be capitalized. This is intentional on my part. It is my way of drawing attention to the importance of the words themselves. Pay attention. Trust. Change. Let Love In. And then, let Love Out.

walking toward the
stairway of
understanding allows us
to go deep within
to climb the
stairway to the stars

Elaine M. Grohman

6

THE POWER OF POWER

*"Don't go around saying
the world owes you a living;
the world owes you nothing;
it was here first."*

Mark Twain

Spirit Message

*"Dear Friends, We stand by your side, each and every moment
of your lives, and it is our greatest pleasure when you finally recognize the truth of our existence. We stand by your side to comfort
you, to counsel you, to honor you and to love you. We stand by
your side to give your strength, to give you hope, to give you encouragement and to give you Love.*

*Our purpose in your Life is to let you know how incredibly im-
portant you are. You have not and will never be an insignificant
being in this grand world. You are significant beyond your
wildest imaginings.*

*The value that is within your precious heart could never be meas-
ured against all the treasures that one can attain. What is material is insignificant, but what is Spirit is magnificent. You are
Spirit in a material illusion. All that you look upon, touch, attempt to possess is nothing compared to the immeasurable wealth
within you.*

The journey that brought you here is a journey that is just beginning. Each of you has great Power within you, and it is our privilege to help you recognize it. Especially now in this time of human history, women are beginning to comprehend the Power that is inherent within their very DNA.

It is the power to nurture, to bring forth life, to comfort, to blend, to heal, to stand firm in the knowing that it is time for the human race to heal. Women, do not be afraid of the Power that is within you. Within you is the Power to bring Peace to Your world.

Humanity - It is time to release your armaments and stand within the Holy Space of your own Hearts. Release the burdens you have carried and let the sweet Tears of Love flow. Embrace the Power of Love within you and stand in the Strength of your own Goodness.

Allow the Power of Free Will to bring Peace into your Lives. For far too long, man-made, unnatural chains have bound you in the form of rules and laws that do not serve human potential. Abuse by any name is still abuse. Release it from your Lives. Free yourselves from the destruction of false imprisonment in all its varied forms.

There will be those who choose to wound others. Do not fall prey to their illusion of power, but rather, walk away with Peace in your Heart and bless them on your way.

This is the gift of a Lifetime. It is the gift of knowing your own Power. This gift is the Power to be Strong, the Power to be Kind, the Power to Love, and the Power to Forgive. Be a bringer of Peace. Starting with You."

It is clearly time for change. You can look anywhere and see that systems are not supporting Life. The financial systems, the health care system, the educational system all have mounting problems that seem to continue without much relief. The problem is that we have abdicated our own Power to be Self-limiting, Self-governing and Self-responsible. We have looked in the direction of what we want, rather than look at the problems immediately at hand. Many things that we hold as images of power are actually images of abuse. The Power that is being conveyed by Spirit is a Power of a much different kind.

Let's take a look at some of our systems that abuse power – to the detriment of humanity.

Long before Wall Street's prestigious image was tarnished, it had been a beacon of stability and might - a symbol of financial power. The abuse of that power is all too fresh in our memory. Formulated to be a beacon of stability and might it became a hiding place of corruption and greed.

Few of us know that there was an actual wall constructed with the express purpose of keeping the Native People known as the Lenape from reclaiming the land in which they lived. European settlers gave the Lenape goods in exchange for the help that had been given. Unfortunately the Lenape did not realize that the "goods" were equivalent to a purchase in the eyes of the Europeans. This is where Wall Street is today.(1)

It was inconceivable to the Lenape that anyone could own the land, as they believed it was merely ours to care for and enjoy while we are here.

Force is not the same as Power. In the Native tradition, the word

Power means Gift. Not the kind of gifts that we are accustomed to accumulating, but a Gift of Responsibility. Anyone who had a Power recognized the Gift and Responsibility inherent in the care of that Power. Abuse of that Power would be unthinkable, since it was known that Spirit is aware of our breath before we take it.

We are being asked to rethink what is meant by Power. Let's look further into other instances in our history where power has been corrupted.

The problem of power became dramatic and dangerous with the onset of religion. The word "religion" comes from the Latin word *"religare"* which means "to bind or restrain".

Taken at face value, to "restrain" implies limitations, which if un-heeded could lead to punishment and death. We don't need to look far to see how the power that religions have claimed has caused untold hardship, torture and criminal behavior. Many re-ligions have made women the enemy of man and often sub-human. This is an abuse of power.

Power used well brings about Balance. Balance is a Measure of how we are willing to be, act and use the Gift of Power for the betterment of all.

---

1. Taken from History Confidential – Morsels of Little Known History Facts

http://www.historyconfidential.com/2009/06/the-origin-of-wall-street

FALLING AWAY

*"When you have faults,
do not fear
to abandon them."*

Confucius

551 - 479 B.C.

Spirit Message
October 14, 2009

"As the weather changes, you are being given a visual reminder that there are times when things must be allowed to fall away. The magnificent trees have shared their beauty with humanity, bringing shade in the heat of the day and the soothing sounds of wind through their branches. Now they express the beauty of color and share a glimpse of their special gifts before quietly preparing for winter's sleep.

Nature is constantly giving examples of renewal, of appreciating the new, and of savoring its wonder and then letting it fade.

Like Nature's cycles, we ask you to effortlessly begin to allow your old woundings to fall away. Times gone by can be treasured in your memories or they can be held captive in your mind. Which do you choose?

Past transgressions that you have witnessed or participated in need to be released so that new growth, new ideas, and new wonder can take its place in your Life..

Like autumn, it is time to let things fall away. No longer hold onto things, memories, emotions or judgments that do not serve your highest good. Let them fall to the Earth, to be reabsorbed so that in the coming seasons you can reflect upon what you have learned and await the beauty that lies before you."

———————————

The sensations of the cool autumn breeze mingled with the warmth of the sun coexist within my being. Within the space of seemingly contrasting sensations a third sensation emerges - I feel Peace.

Healing begins in the same way; the opposing forces of fear and relief, pain and relaxation, doubt and contentment, anger and forgiveness all come to a place of balance and equilibrium when we let go. When we hold fast to the illusion that we have control of our lives, sooner or later Life will let us know that we are not in charge. It is in the wonderful moment of acknowledging that we don't know that Creation can present us with a solution, a healing or a release.

I have struggled many times trying to determine what has gone wrong, all the while failing to notice what I have forgotten to release. Holding onto what we think we "should" do sets us up for heartache and disappointment. The problem that we face is not what happens to us but how we react to what happens to us.

Often the greatest examples of letting go are right outside our window. Nature gives us beautiful examples on a daily basis of the cycles of renewal, release and rebirth, if only we would stop long enough to witness it. Many of the answers we seek appear when we ask the right questions, and often the answers are staring us in the face.

Throughout the seasons we witness nature as it flows from one cycle to the next. Springtime brings emerging life as seedlings tenaciously push the dirt aside, reaching for the warmth of the sun. Seemingly overnight the Earth is alive with buzzing insects and brilliant, fragrant flowers in every imaginable shade, fragrance and texture. Seeds that have been planted will soon share their bounty with us, sustaining our lives now and in the coming seasons.

Quietly, the energy spent in such rapid production begins to wane, giving way to the splendor of autumn. The balance of warm days and cool nights trigger a kaleidoscope of colors that splash across the landscape, all the more brilliant against the crystal blue sky. Everything in Nature is in balance.

The beautiful leaves release themselves from their home in the sky to fall softly to Earth, not struggling to stay longer than is meant to be. Leaves decay in order to enhance the growing environment of next season's plants. Slowly winter comes. And the cycle goes on.

We would do well to follow Nature's lead. Nurture your own environment to ensure that your Life will blossom when it is time to blossom and when it is Time to Let go, bless future generations with the work that you have done.

LOVE IS WHO YOU ARE

"Greater than the tread
of mighty armies
is an idea whose time has come."

Victor Hugo 1802-1885

Spirit Message
October 26, 2009

"Friends, know that your precious hearts are the gift that you have been waiting for. You no longer have to wait for the moment to arrive to begin to enjoy your Life. You have waited for days upon days to begin to live and the moment is truly now. The gift that this awareness will bring to your Life will be the gift of a Lifetime. In fact, it is the gift of all of your Lifetimes, and that gift is Love.

Love is the essence of your Being. Love is what you do and who you are. You may wish to pause for a moment to comprehend this fact. Love is not something that happens to You. Love is Who and what You are. It is the spark that brings a sparkle to your eyes, a beat to your heart and a breath to your Life.

As you begin to seek the comfort of the warmth of your own hearth in the cool days ahead, know that the warmth that has any lasting effect is the warmth that you have for yourself and all beings – all things and all moments.

The warmth that brings deep and lasting comfort is the warmth of your own Love for yourself. When Love is present everything else will take care of itself. There is nothing else to have or give. Just Be Love, and all will be well in your world."

Life brings us many opportunities to grow, change, love and learn. Not all of these lessons are easily won nor are they always understood while one is embroiled in the experience. Yet, the lessons will surely come, and we should be grateful for the learning.

One such opportunity took place at my sister's home on the shores of Lake Huron. It was Memorial Day weekend. It was one thirty in the morning. The air was heavy with moisture from the days and days of rain and the cool evening air caused everyone's breath to be seen, like soft lights momentarily suspended in the darkness.

Observing and listening to young adults as they reminisce about their childhood helps us to better understand their own unique vantage points. Their recall of events may differ from your own, which only serves to emphasize the unique perspectives that make us individuals. We view the world through our own lenses, and as parents we hope those lenses have the soft glow of love's influence.

Sitting in the darkness I listened to their reminiscing and witnessed my own flashing memories mingled with the emotions those memories evoked. Newlyweds, brothers and sisters, nieces, nephews, boyfriends and girlfriends shared their precious memories. Some may have thought that they were simply listening to stories. I heard insights and deep thoughts, some more telling than others.

The laughter and the sweet time of being together in the dark night brought me to the realization of the palpable presence of Love. Whether we know it or not, we are constantly making memories, and hopefully, good ones. In the warmth of our conversation, new memories were created. Listening carefully I could hear the strength of self-knowing in some and the crippling moments of self-doubt in others.

It is up to us to teach Self Love to our children. Self Love is not selfish, but rather a deep comfort that can be found in goodness. Goodness is not always rewarded, but it can be the building blocks of the foundation of self-regulation, self-awareness and self-responsibility.

My grown children began telling stories of their childhood friend, Bonzo the Wonder Dog. They grew up under his watchful eye, his ever present shaggy softness, and the warm glow from his eyes helped them to know that they were always safe when he was around. Bonzo showed his love by being their ever-vigilant guardian and often, nap mate. Animals are wonderful teachers to humankind as they naturally exude Love.

The simple gift of memories can be poignant lessons of friendship and trust. Listen to your children, no matter their age, and dare to be silent so that you may learn more about them and your influence in their lives. Do not defend or be unwilling to hear... Listen and learn.

BE THE DESTINATION

"Little by little
the times goes by,
short if you sing it,
long if you sigh."

Anonymous

Spirit Message
November 12, 2009
3:51 pm

"Dearest Friends, we wish to speak to you this day about con-
cerns that are heard in all dimensions of time, emanating from
the hearts of humanity. 'Where do we go from here? What should
I do now? What is my next step?' These questions plague your
hearts and minds.

What if you knew that there is no "there" that you must get to,
nor a destination that you should be striving for? For that is the
truth of the matter. There is no place that you must be, no place
that you must rush to and no place where you must go. It is the
running towards something else that preoccupies your mind, clut-
ters your thoughts and blinds you from the greatest destination
you could ever seek.

What if you were to ask yourself another question, "Who shall I

BE now?" It is not a matter of going to, but rather a matter of BEING. There is no destination more important than to step into the chambers of your own heart and to sit in quiet contemplation of all that is there for you to embrace. There is no greater treasure or any destination more captivating than to BE YOURSELF. Only you can express who you are.

This does not mean that you should prohibit yourself from enjoying the opportunity to "visit" certain locations, for there are boundless examples of beauty and wonder upon this planet. No, enjoy the wonders that have been created for all to enjoy. Seek the wonder of nature, the beauty of the stars and the sweet, soft breath of a sleeping child. At that moment allow yourself to experience the wonder of BEING YOU. Not another being in the whole of humanity - past, present or future - can experience the wonder of you. That is your own precious gift.

Do not seek a destination, rather, be a constant expression of Love in the heart of humanity. This will help you to see the incredible gift of Life. Express yourself each and every day with the Love that is your truest treasure and your greatest destination. It is the very purpose of your birth. Bring Love wherever you go and the destination you seek will be in every step you take."

Humanity struggles every day to conform to prescribed roles that we believe we must play. Every culture has created particular roles for each of the sexes, some implied, some overt and some demanded. These roles have prevented most from being their truest selves, their most genuine selves. Societies have pushed others to conform to man made guidelines that have brought untold harm to the human heart, mind and often, body.

Countless times people have asked, "What should I do now?" or "What is my Life's purpose?" and the answer is always the same. Believe it or not we each have exactly the same Life Purpose and that Life Purpose is to know how to give and receive Love. Love for Nature, Love for one another and Love for ourselves. People think that they know love, but we rarely do. We know the concept of, "I will love you when," or "I will love you if," the conditional baiting of love, as if love was a commodity that can be bartered. Love, in its purest sense is what WE are MADE of. Denial of the very essence of our Being is what stops Love in its tracks.

Hate and anger are not the opposite of Love but the denial of Love. To deny Love is to deny Life itself. So often we are confronted by our angers and fears, never really stopping to look at the cause of this distress. The cause of human anger and suffering is the denial of Love.

The subject of love has been written about perhaps more than any other topic, whether in poem, prose or music, but it eludes us because we don't know it. It eludes us because we deny it. It eludes us because we forget where it must begin. Love must begin within us. Standing firmly in that understanding allows pretense to drop away. We want love but we don't love. And therein lies the problem. Love is a give and take, an expression of giving and receiving thousands of times a day and in a thousand ways.

Where do we go from here? We begin with LOVE. We must begin IN Love with Love as the starting point and we do not reach the finish line until the end of our days.

"To Love your neighbor AS yourself," is an invitation to look

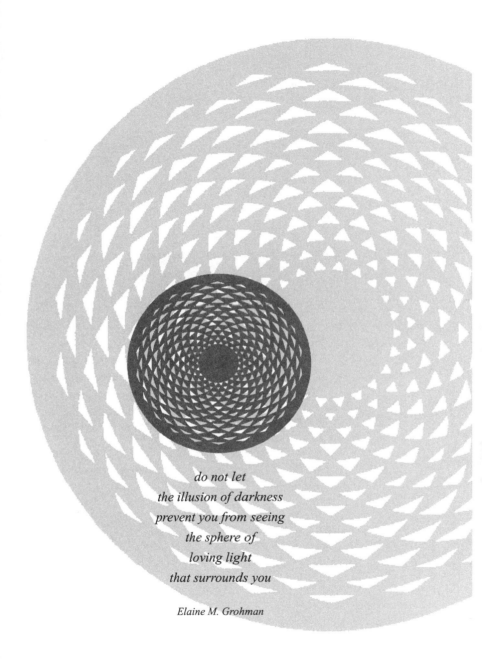

*do not let
the illusion of darkness
prevent you from seeing
the sphere of
loving light
that surrounds you*

Elaine M. Grohman

within to see where Love must first be recognized and employed. To love yourself is not a selfish act, but rather an awareness that if we care for ourselves first, we will be more capable of caring for one another.

More times than I wish to count, I have denied my own feelings, my own knowing, and my own Love, in an attempt to conform to what I "should" do. It has never brought joy, hope or peace, only discontent. It was only when I started to let Love Live in me that tension began to lose its hold on my own heart and my life's journey began to unfold before me. It wasn't magic, although it is magical. It was mysterious and wonderful and fun. It was simply Love at work in and through my Life. Let Love guide you and Love will bring Goodness to you. It can be no other way.

THANKS GIVING

"Our grand business in life
is not to see what lies dimly
at a distance,
but to do what lies clearly at hand."

Thomas Carlyle 1795-1881

Book signing event at Farmington Civic Theater
Spirit Message
Thursday, November 19, 2009
7:44 am

"Thanks giving, Thanks giving.... Thanks giving. The true gift that you can give one another and yourselves each and every day is Thanks giving. Giving thanks for all that you have is an act of wonder, an act of kindness, an act of stillness and an act of Love.

This human world is greatly in need of Thanks giving. Thanks giving is the act of acknowledging all that you have, all that surrounds you, all that helps you grow, all that brings awareness into your life. The sorrows and the disappointments, the trials and the triumphs...all need your thanks in order to be understood. Acknowledge the importance of every Human Being.

Thanks giving. What are you truly thank-full for?

Anger robs you of precious Time and may appear to stem from injury, illness, or life's circumstances. Left unchecked, anger will erode your happiness and blind you to the potential gifts of awareness that every Life situation holds. Even if one thinks they hide their anger well, it is more visible than one might imagine.

Do not bring anger where you wish to have health. Never for a moment hate an illness, but rather, Love your body. The vibration and the frequency of Love will cause a chain reaction within the system, and the situation that is immersed in Love will change.

You cannot change a diseased body with hate, only Love. You cannot change a broken system with anger, but only with Love. You cannot bring vitality into depression with hate, only with Love. You cannot see the wonder of future possibilities if you hate your present circumstances; only Love supplies the wonder to look joyfully at what is to come.

Learn from every encounter, every smile and every heartache... pay attention to every interaction. Each moment is an opportunity to live in the awareness of Thanks giving, and when you do your world will surely change.

When you neglect to give thanks, you neglect to acknowledge Life. When you neglect to acknowledge Life, all you see is lack. Lack is the denial of Love. Bring Love Forth. Be an act of Thanks giving. Thank yourself, thank others, thank nature for its beauty, thank struggle as it helps you learn your strengths. Live the act of Thanks giving.

There will be experiences that bring you concern, whether on a global scale or an interpersonal one. When a relationship comes to a standstill, give thanks for what you have learned - most im-

portantly about yourself - and then release it from your heart and allow the process of healing to begin. At times it is necessary to walk away from the disturbances in order that Peace may be restored to your Heart. Do not judge, rather, observe, learn, change, grow and then Give Thanks.

It is all too easy to look at something and misinterpret the gift in the experience.

Give thanks and be Happy in your Thanks giving. It is the Gift of Love and it has the Power to Change Everything!"

The evening of Thursday, November 19, 2009 was an event I had only dreamed of. The amazing thing was that the dream had come true. I was about to give my very first lecture and book signing for my book, *The Angels and Me*. Everything had beautifully fallen into place in ways that took my breath away.

I had chosen the venue, The Civic Theater, for sentimental reasons. The Civic was the very first movie theatre I had ever been to when I was just five years old. It has that classic charm of an old time movie theatre that the mega movie complexes will never have. Standing outside the theater doors I gazed up to see my name and book title on the marquee. Literally, my name was in lights. I have to admit, it was very cool.

Writing the book was an emotional journey, and once the book was complete I wondered how I would get the money to get it printed. "Just get it written," was the loving prod. One by one those worries faded. Soon I would be standing on the stage speaking to whoever decided to show. I was nervous and excited all at the same time.

Early that morning I asked Spirit to provide a message for the audience. It was appropriate that Their message was about Thanks Giving. It was not only because the Thanksgiving holiday was one week away, but the whole notion of Thanks Giving was so wonderfully evident that day.

Through laughter and tears the evening was everything that I had hoped for. An afterglow followed with family and friends.

The evening was magical, miraculous and just plain fun. And one of my worries had been lifted off of my shoulders. Not only were all of my expenses for the book covered that evening, but also I was able to share my heartfelt thanks with those who had supported me. My hope was to let others know that they could do it too. Giving Thanks is powerful stuff.

BE

*"Every situation - nay,
every moment - is of infinite worth;
for it is the representative
of a whole eternity."*

Johann Wolfgang Von Goethe

Spirit Message
December 10, 2009
5:09 pm

"Tis the Season to Be... Tis the Season to Be... Tis the Season to BE.

The refrain of this song has greater meaning than you currently know. It is often understood, when looking with fresh eyes, and hearing with innocent ears, that messages of great importance are hidden in plain sight, and in this case, in the lyrics of a Christmas Carol.

Tis the Season to be... Tis the Season to BE... Tis the Season to BE...

It is this season, in which many are caught up in the excitement of the holiday season, that many neglect to take into their hearts the real meaning of this time of year. It is not only the time in which humankind celebrates the birth of your brother, Jesus of Nazareth, but also the time of appreciating all that is within the Seasons of your Life. The Seasons of your Life are indeed every moment that you breathe and exist upon this beautiful planet.

In the awareness of those moments, begin to grasp the true meaning of the message of the song, "Tis the Season." Right now, at this very moment, know that it is the Season to Be...whatever you choose.

Do you choose to be happy, or do you choose to be afraid? Do you choose to be grateful, or do you choose to believe that there is not enough to go around? Do you choose to look into the eyes of others and see yourself staring back at you, or do you see another whom you believe is different from you? Tis the Season, our dear friends, to Be Joyful, Loving, Compassionate, Forgiving, Quiet, Still, Dancing, Humble and at Peace.

It is and has always been your most precious gift, the gift of choice. So when you hear that Christmas Carol, regardless of the season in which you are living, recall the true meaning of "Tis the Season" to Be... Be Your Greatest Self in every minute of every day, and This Season, This Life, will have been a celebration of the Season of Wonder and Love."

Sometimes it seems that Life is full of irony, especially when someone who has done everything right gets sick. They are physically fit, and always have been. They are conscientious about food that they eat and just about everything else that is meant to promote health. And they get sick anyway.

When people get sick it isn't uncommon for them to wonder, "What did I do wrong?"

It is wise to recognize that illness will come at some point in life. The problem is not that we get sick, but how we respond when we do. There are so many factors that influence our health, but one factor that is often overlooked is our way of Being. What you might have forgotten is that you have a choice.

When we have habitual responses to life's events, we often neglect to recognize the consequences of our responses. A whole host of chemical reactions occur when we get upset or angry. Without our thinking, a chain reaction of chemicals is released in the body that can further escalate our reactions. Anger creates anger…and Peace creates Peace.

The Power of our Choice can change things, defusing resentment, anger and a need to be "right" and offer in its place a time of reflection and insight. A peaceful mind and heart can open the door for wonderful things to happen…even if health cannot be regained.

Choices can allow us time for reflection and insight and hopefully the Peace to make better choices from that moment on. Make your choices count so that you can add Beauty to your days.

I would like to share a story with you. I was the Volunteer Services Manager at a large hospice organization. It was my job to recruit, train and place volunteers with patients and their families. I also wanted to educate the public about hospice care and I thought it might be great to start with kids. By bringing kids into the hospice home before they experienced a family death might help them to understand that dying is a part of living.

I invited a local middle school music class to come and play for the patients. The kids were excited. The day of the scheduled "concert" I asked the patients if they would like to have the kids play for them – right at their bedside.

One woman in particular, I'll call her Mary, was excited to have the kids come to play for her. They entered her room with instruments in hand and formed a semi-circle around her bed. Beautifully off-key, they began to play. Mary's frail body momentarily came to life as her eyes shone with Love and appreciation for their music, their youth and their Love. Mary beamed at the conclusion of her private musical interlude. Without making a sound she brought her frail hands together and silently clapped in gratitude. She whispered her thanks and asked that I return once the children had gone.

I returned to her room as promised and she asked if I would read to her from her Daily Prayer book. She closed her eyes and listened to the prayer. When she opened her eyes we looked at one another and I asked, "Mary, how do you feel about what is happening to you?" Sweetly, her youth shone from her ninety year old eyes. "I am so grateful for each and every day. I am ready to die, Elaine, but I don't want it to be too soon. After all, I never know on what day I will meet the person that God has sent me here to meet. I wouldn't want to miss that opportunity." She brought tears to my eyes.

Mary was an example of an individual who appreciated Life and all that it brought her. She had made the choice to Live each and every day with an open, joyful heart. I am sure that in her ninety years she had seen much, yet at the end of the day she was grateful to BE.

each soul evolves
every moment is an opportunity
to choose
who you wish to be
is that choice kind
loving
truthful
or is it
afraid that there is
nothing but the
patterns that have been
established by the self
step into the central circle
and know that you
are already whole
make your choices worthwhile

Elaine M. Grohman

Shine Your Light

*"Opportunity is missed by most people
because it is dressed in overalls
and looks like work."*

Thomas Edison

Spirit Message
December 16, 2009
5:20 pm

*"Dear Friends, it is time for you to know why you are here. Why
you have chosen to be here at this most amazing time in the history of humankind. You have chosen to live with your eyes open,
with your minds open and with your hearts open.*

*There have been times in your life when you have been harsh with
yourself and others, and we tell you with great conviction that
this should be no more. It is time to Shine Your Light on those
with whom you live, work, love and encounter. It is time for you
to Be a Light for the World to See.*

*You may feel that this is beyond you, and we tell you it is not be-
yond you. It is within you. Know this as we know it, and you will
no longer fritter away your precious time in meaningless pursuits.
Let anger fall away. Let resentment fall away. Let judgment fall
away. No longer wait for something to change. Change comes*

from within you.

We ask that you begin to listen to the longings of your own heart. And when you know that you have allowed your Light to dim, if even for a second, all is not lost. State to yourself, to Creation and to the entire Universe that you will judge no more. That truly is and will be the Last Judgment.

When you knowingly shine your Light on every situation, person or memory in your life, you bring about a clarity that can change everything.

Humanity, no longer waste the beauty of your existence on anything that is less than Love. Let goodness shine forth and your path will be illuminated by your own goodness. Then you will begin to see the goodness within yourself and others.

Only when you cease judgment can clarity be presented to you. Stop judging yourselves and others harshly, and the Melody of Life will sing with every breath that you take. Shine your Light, dear friends, Shine your Light."

Have you ever been around a person who makes you feel good just by being with them? I hope so. I know that I have. There are people in this world who have a sparkle about them, a Light that shines from their eyes and hearts that brings joy into a room, into a conversation and even into quiet times together. It is such a blessing when that happens.

What is different about someone like that? Really, only one thing.

They enjoy being Alive. That does not mean that they don't have problems or challenges in their lives. We all do. What is unique about them is that they look beyond the challenges and don't allow the challenges to rob them of their passion for Life and Living.

I am blessed to have someone like that in my life, and I have for my entire life. Her name is Judith Ann, and she is my sister. She is Number 1 in our family, in more ways than one. She is also known lovingly as "The Queen." But she is the kind of queen who has no subjects – rather, you become the subject of her attention, encouragement and love.

Let me tell you a little something about her. Each and every time she calls me on the phone this is what I hear, "Good Morning, Sunshine," or "Hi Sunshine, it's Judy!" Can you imagine how that makes me feel? I'll tell you how it makes me feel... like a million bucks!

I have been blessed throughout my life with living examples of people who "Shine" with effortless displays of Love, Humility and Joy. Ever since I was a little girl, I could count on her sweetness. She has always been an example of Living Life, no matter what life brings. Never once has she ever said something unkind to me. Not ever. I have said it before, and I will say it again, "Everyone should be blessed with a Judy!" And I mean it.

Find yourself a Judy, or better yet, be one yourself. It isn't all that hard to be kind and thoughtful, it just takes a little practice.

The best part of our sisterhood is that she has taught me how to be a better person – what more could you hope for? Thanks, Sunshine! That is why she is "The Queen."

it is impossible
to be out of reach
when you stretch your arms
out toward love

Elaine M. Grohman

BE LOVED

"You do not need to leave your room.
Remain sitting at your table and listen.
Do not even listen, simply wait.
Do not even wait, be quite still and solitary.
The world will freely offer itself to you to be unmasked,
it has no choice, it will roll in ecstasy at your feet."

Franz Kafka

Spirit Message
January 21, 2010
2:14 pm

"It is always a blessing to both Heaven and Earth when you be-
come aware of us, your Divine Friends and travelers on this jour-
ney of your Life. It is the most heartfelt desire of all of God's
Creation that you recognize that you have a Choice in all that
you do.

Life is marked by tiny segments of Time that give you the oppor-
tunity to become aware of who You are. Each precious moment
is a Lifetime within itself for truly you do not know when your
journey will end. This simple acknowledgment will bring you
great clarity and each and every second will be precious and
magical. No other single being can express your Life. This is
your Gift. This is your opportunity.

We witness the tragic loss of this Gift throughout the world as people grasp their wounds and hold them fast. The simple act of letting go releases you from the illusion of separation and limitations. It is you alone who limits you.

We ask that you look beyond the reality of your physical body or your physical presence in a particular location upon the Earth to truly become aware of who you ARE.

You are a magnificent Creation... an expression of the Love of God. By your very existence you are showing the world that God's Love is the most potent power imaginable. It is time for you to recognize that you, as a Creation of God, have the ability to command the Love that IS you to be present at all times in your Life.

Allow yourself to begin to comprehend the Power that is within your own Heart. For you, too, are Creators. You create your own reality each and every day. This does not mean that you have control of the physical forces around you, yet you have great influence in your physical world. Soon science will understand the radiant Light that emanates from the Human Heart and Body and comprehend how to direct that Light for the betterment of Mother Earth and all of Her inhabitants.

You are 100% in control of your inner forces.... the force that can change humanity in an instant - the Force of your Love.

You bring Love into your world by Being Love. You become the Gift to humanity. You become the Gift of compassion. You become the expression of non-judgment. You are more powerful than you have ever been willing to recognize. This great Gift of Love is the most valuable possession that you can fathom.

38

In an instant you can BE an Expression of Love by the Power of your own Heart. Love holds no one bound. Love releases and controls no one. Humanity is now seeking to understand Love as an Energy and Power - not as an emotional tool of manipulation. No man or woman can hold you bound without your consent. Do not consent to this personal violence.

Humanity has created rules that have no bearing in the Heart of Creation. Create YOUR Life and release yourselves from limited thinking and self-imposed restrictions that are based upon the judgment of others. It is better to walk away penniless with the blessing of Love in your heart than to stay imprisoned in hate surrounded by the illusion of riches.

No longer judge the life of another with contempt and swift abandon. As you see ANY suffering around you ask that Love come Forth. In fact, Command it to be Present through your Presence. Your brother and fellow human, the man known as Jeshua, or in your language, Jesus, was a shining example of this Essence and His awareness of the Command of Love.

By many he has been called, "The Beloved," and it is time for you to be "The Beloved" also. Being "Beloved" does not set you apart from others but draws you nearer to your own Soul, to the Purpose of your Existence, to understanding the very Reason for Your Life. Look at the word again, and change your concept of unworthiness to the reality of your Truth, BELOVED...BE LOVED... and all things around you will BE LOVED by your presence."

I had the privilege of having a dear, gifted Medicine Man speak with great clarity and love to me. He told me in no uncertain terms that I had to let go of my anger. I was shocked. I thought that I had. But the truth was that he could see what I did not want to see. I was angry and it wasn't helping one single bit – and in fact, it was hurting me in more ways than one. And the truth was that he was right, I hadn't let it go and I knew it.

I thought about his statement for quite some time. It was hard to get it out of my mind, especially when my anger flared, even if momentarily - even if no one else saw it. I could feel it and each time I was reminded of the poison of that emotion. Each time I felt anger rise in me it caused me to pause and take a look at it. You have to study your anger to really understand it. By studying it you can look at your anger without being angry… and you just might learn something.

What I learned was that it was my choice to be angry or not, regardless of the situation I found myself in. I did not need to follow old patterns. I did not need to defend myself or justify my anger. I just needed to look at it so that I could change my point of view. This realization brought me closer and closer to being more peaceful, less reactionary and more able to let Love have its place more fully in me.

And then one day I had an experience that showed me the Power that Love has within us. Let me share with you what happened.

I have a precious friend named Meg whom I have known since first grade. Throughout our lives together we have had experiences of "tapping into" one another's thoughts. Many, many times during our younger days before there were cell phones and caller ID, when the phone would ring I would somehow "know" that it was Meg calling. I would simply answer the phone saying, "Hello Meg," and invariably she would laugh and we both would be mildly shocked, though not surprised. There were many times that I would be the one calling Meg, and she would answer her phone by saying, "Hi Lanes." We always got a kick out of that, and still do. Now we have cell phones that announce the caller, which kind of takes the fun out of it.

Meg and her husband John moved from Michigan to California in order to be closer to their sons. It just so happened that Meg was coming home to visit family and invited me to join them for a few days in northern Michigan.

There is always so much to catch up on but we always take the time to steal way and talk about what is really important in our lives. We have deep discussions about what we are experiencing and what it might be all about.

We took a walk on the beach and admired the beauty of Lake Michigan. The stones were like jewels on the sand and the wind shared the coolness of the air with us. I talked to Meg about my experiences with the Medicine Man and deep in my heart I could feel the overwhelming sadness that had triggered my anger. I wanted to be done with it, yet I did not want to loose the lesson that Spirit was trying to share through my stubbornness.

As we walked and talked, I recall telling her that I didn't want to hold that anger any longer and I prayed that it would be released from me. Literally, in the next step as I watched my foot touch the wet sand, I felt a "whoosh" of Energy flood my body, as if someone had stood by me and dumped a bucket of warm water from head to toe. This Energy flooded through me. In the next step I felt an incredible Lightness, as if the Energy has washed the residue of anger from me and simply let it blend with the water at my feet, allowing it to be lost in the enormity of the lake. I felt relief. I felt joy. I felt Loved.

And it all happened with my friend Meg by my side. That is the beauty of friendship. You get to Be Loved.

YOUR SACRED HEART

"Life is a series of inspired follies.
The difficulty is to find them to do.
Never lose a chance:
it doesn't come every day."

George Bernard Shaw

Spirit Message
March 10, 2010
4:15 pm

"It is you. It is you. It is you...

You are the one who is needed to bring Peace to this world. You are the one who is needed to bring comfort to humanity. You are the one who is needed to be a bringer of Peace.

It is you, our precious friends, who are needed so very much. Peace cannot come from another place, another time... another dimension. Peace must come from YOU.

Deep within your body is a place of incredible Power and Light, and that place is your own Sacred Heart. Your Sacred Heart is the doorway to unbridled Love and Compassion. It is the doorway to Peace and Harmony. It is the doorway of Miracles. For you see, it is You who has the ability to Bring Love to this Earth unlike any other.

Only YOU can bring the Love that you are to every second of your Life. It is YOU who can choose forgiveness, YOU who can choose compassion, YOU who can choose to look within and know that this untapped resource can come pouring from your being and heal the wounded hearts of others.

It is you, dear friends, whose importance can no longer be denied and whose life's purposes can no longer be silenced.

It is you that is needed to bring Peace. It is YOU!

Your Sacred Heart is an untapped reservoir of the healing balm called Love. For a moment, bring your attention to this holy place within you. Invite Love to come forth to bring Love and Blessings to all that you know and all that you do."

I had the privilege of meeting an individual who truly understood that each and every life could make a difference. Her example touched millions and I am fortunate to say that I am one of those millions.

My stepmother Jane had been a long time friend of Mother Teresa. Yes, *the* Mother Teresa. They had met in the early 1960's and remained friends until Mother Teresa's death. In the early 1970's, Jane brought her to Detroit and I had the privilege of standing on the same stage as she addressed the crowd in the Grand Ballroom of Detroit's Cobo Hall. I was amazed at how powerful she was even though she was very small in stature. She had a dignity and holiness that was palpable. It seemed as though nothing and no one intimidated this little one.

In October 2003 my stepmother Jane, my stepsister Therese and I made the trip to Rome for the beatification of her friend, Mother Teresa. At eighty-three and wheelchair bound, Jane was determined to make the trip, knowing full well that it was probably her last.

The Beatification Mass took place at St. Peter's Square in Rome on October 19, 2003. The events of that morning were nothing short of remarkable. The closer we got to the entrance of St. Peter's Square the more crowded it became. It was expected that 500,000 people would be in attendance that day. With Jane in her wheelchair, Therese and I had great concern for her safety. Her tiny frame was crippled from arthritis, and the least push or bump would cause terrible pain. We literally used our bodies as physical shields in an attempt to protect her.

As we inched closer to the entry gate, the passageway was getting narrower and people began pushing one another in their desperation to get into the square. An older Italian gentleman noticed our concern and immediately both he and his son began to speak in Italian to the people surrounding us asking them to be careful.

The older gentleman attempted to get the attention of the Vatican police who were guarding the entryway, but they were just out of hearing distance and the crowd was too loud to be heard above. I yelled to Therese asking her to whistle as loud as she could. As she did, her whistle was loud enough to cause one of the police officers to look our way. He looked directly at me as I attempted to indicate that there was someone in a wheelchair and that we needed help.

Within a few moments it was as if the Red Sea had parted. Officers started to move people aside while I continued to protect Jane with my body, trying to prevent her from being crushed. The crowd was so thick that people were passing out. It was not a pleasant situation.

Seeing the panic in my eyes, the officers escorted us to the entrance and literally had to lift Jane, wheelchair and all, over the metal barricade. I never let go of her wheelchair or my sister Therese's hand as we struggled to stay together. As we were passing through, one of the guards told us in Italian that only one of us would be allowed to go to Jane. "No," I pleaded, "this is my sister, she has to come with us." Had we been separated it would have been virtually impossible for us to find one another. Hearing the panic in my voice the guard allowed us all to go through the entry together. Once safely on the other side we held each other and sobbed.

Once through the entry we had plenty of space to move and we made our way into the main area of St. Peter's Square. There we discovered another problem. There were so many people that it would have been impossible for Jane to see anything. I thought, "This is not good." I was determined that Jane was going to be able to see this event. I asked Therese to stay with Jane and I made my way over to another barricaded area.

Police and security guards stood behind the barricade keeping a very large walkway clear. I walked as far as I could and made eye contact with one of the police officers. I motioned to him that I had someone in a wheelchair. Would it be possible for us to get through to a safer area? Without being able to speak the language, amazingly I was able to get my point across. One by one the guards relayed the message. "Let them in. Let them in," as they pointed us out to one another. These gentlemen not only let us in, but personally escorted us to an amazing spot, right under the sculpture of an Angel. Ask and you shall receive.

Although rain was in the forecast it could not have been a more beautiful day. The sun was shining and the sky was bright blue. In fact, it began to get so hot that the Vatican guards and security personnel began passing out thousands of bottles of water. What an amazing thing to witness.

The event was joyous, as the spirit of this powerful little human being was honored. I think that she would not have wanted to have such a fuss made over her. She was living the life that she had always wanted, to serve the poor, and in so doing she was an example of love, courage, grace and strength far beyond her diminutive frame.

To say that this trip was a remarkable is an understatement. I am grateful to have had the opportunity to have such an extraordinary experience. We were truly blessed to be there. Mother Teresa was a living example that every person can make a difference. She recognized the Power of the Love within her own Sacred Heart. If she could do it, couldn't we?

KINDNESS

"You cannot do a kindness too soon,
for you never know
how soon it will be too late."

Ralph Waldo Emerson

Spirit Message
March 19, 2010
8:18 am

"Be kind to yourself. Please... be kind to yourself.

It is understood that you are expected to be kind to others, yet the most important person in your life is often neglected. Please, be kind to yourself.

It is the care of the self that we wish to speak about. Humanities greatest disease is judgment. It has been the cause of years of heartache, untold conflict, and ultimately battles - all waged against the self within the human heart. The time is now. You must begin to be kind to yourself.

This human journey is the opportunity, literally of a Lifetime, to finally see the grander picture, the broader view, while at the same time looking within the chambers of your own Precious Heart, the Sacred Center in which your soul resides.

Please do not misunderstand. The soul, your soul, is not separate from you, but in truth is the complete and utter perfection of you. It does not exist outside of you, but rather in the inner most chambers of your Sacred Self...Your Sacred Heart. It is a place of pure existence, of pure wonder, of pure joy, of pure Love and of pure creation. It is where you are from, what you are and who you express yourself as... LOVE. You are nothing but Love.

Be kind to yourself in thought, word and deed. Any time you find yourself seeing less than your own perfection, stop, look within, and know that you are Love, expressing who you are in every moment. From moments of quiet sleep, to deep contemplation, to joyful banter, to thoughtful conversation - you are expressing YOU.

When humanity, when you, begin to embrace this awareness of Reality, there will be nothing hidden from you. Truly, when you are kind to yourself, you would never harm another in thought, word or action. Be the healing presence that you are. Express love for yourself and you will graciously and willingly share that love with others.

In that way, you will understand the deeper meaning behind the words, "Love one another as I have loved you." Do this willingly, lovingly, openly, joyfully... constantly. And you will know the truth of you, as we, your constant companions, know you... As Love."

There are no coincidences in Life. I know that this is True. Life presents us with examples of how the choices we make are the keys to our empowerment and Peace. Weekly I have conversations with people who are struggling to make sense of events in their lives, usually events in which they feel victimized. We fall into the trap of believing that we must defend ourselves, holding tight to our wounds as if they define us, rather than letting the wounds heal so that Peace can be in its place.

What we often fail to recognize is that our problems can be the impetus for change. The desire for change can be the incentive that spawns new understanding, new relationships and lasting peace. Yet most of us, particularly in the United States, have no idea what it means to really struggle for survival. Yes, many have lost their homes and their jobs, but few of us have ever been faced with the loss of our children's lives and futures or have lived without electricity and running water all the while watching our homeland be destroyed as a result of civil war. It is in the human heart where change begins. In particular, it is within the Hearts of Women, as Keepers of Life, where lasting and meaningful change can be a driving force that forges through adversity. Once that flame is ignited by Love people can come together to end the hardship and restore Life.

Creation reminds us that we are all in this together - that we are our sisters' and brothers' keepers.

We have a family friend by the name of Johnny O. John was in town visiting family and friends during a whirlwind trip before returning home to Nakuru, Kenya. John has lived in Africa for more than three decades. In that time he has established a well drilling business, a leather and silversmith shop all with one goal in mind – self-empowerment and self-sustaining communities.

Johnny O shared an inspirational story of a group of Sudanese women who, ten years ago began to work together, against great odds, to support their children and themselves by creating a fully, women owned company called Lulu Life.(2)

"Lulu" is the Arabic word for the nilotica variety of the shea nut tree that grows prolifically in Southern Sudan. Historically, Sudanese women have been called the "Traditional Guardians" of this tree and its life sustaining nuts and the oil that it produces. The shea nut is not only used for skin care products but it has saved countless people from starvation, as the nut is edible. These amazing trees, a Gift from Creation, grow abundantly and easily survive in drought conditions. It is estimated that the tree can live between 200 and 300 years and will bear fruit after 15 to 20 years.

Through years of civil war, the women of Southern Sudan were stripped of their families, their clothing, their homes and their food and were left to fend for themselves and their children in desperate, dangerous situations. It was the Lulu tree that kept them from starvation and certain death. Under great personal distress, the women of Southern Sudan banded together to support one another and their children in a collaborative effort using the natural resource of the Lulu tree.

An industry was created called Lulu Life that is fully owned and operated by the women of Southern Sudan. The women gather, clean, dry and process the shea nuts to make cooking oil and body products from the nutrient rich shea butter. Through this collaboration they are able to feed, support and educate their families and work together as women to bring health, prosperity and happiness to their communities.

The women of Southern Sudan could easily have become bitter and hopeless, but instead they embraced the understanding of self-love and self-care and are changing their nation by providing opportunities for themselves, their children and all of the women of Mother Earth who are the Traditional Guardians of the Human Heart.

2. To learn more please see "LuLu Life"

http://www.swahiliimports.com/home/si3/page_2986/lulu_life_sudanese_shea_butter_project.html

and watch the powerful documentary entitled, "The Brilliance of Oil".

never stop moving
swirl and laugh
and sing and shout
and dance
with joy
feel the love that is
such a part of your being
let it be felt within you
so that it can
then move you in
the direction
of others
and your dreams

Elaine M. Grohman

YOU ARE KNOWN

*"Creation has a greater knowing
than humanity.
Life is a unique present given individually
to each human born."*

Esteheemah from "Lightningbolt"
by Hyemeyohsts Storm

Spirit Message
April 14, 2010
4:52 pm

"Know this day how important you are. Know this day, that the Love that you are is your signature. Know this day, that it is up to you to be the Shining Light for those around you to see and know.

By being the Light that you are, you help others to recognize their own goodness and that the Source of all Love resides within you as well as every other human being on Mother Earth. Be willing to express your Love as the gift of Humanity's Birthright.

You ARE Love...be it fully."

That says it all.

THE BEAUTIFUL AND MIRACULOUS

*"There is nothing more powerful
than the truth - and often
nothing so strange."*

Daniel Webster

Spirit Message
April 25, 2010
12:57 pm

*"Within the chambers of your heart lies the greatest gift known
to humankind. It is not the gift of wisdom, although this gift will
bring wisdom. It is not the gift of intellect, although this gift will
bring great knowledge. It is not the gift of prophecy, although
this gift will bring you awareness of all plains of existence. The
gift that we are speaking of, is the gift of Love that resides within
the human heart.*

*Humankind has not fully understood the depth and power of the
Love available within the human heart. When actions initiate
from Love, the beautiful and miraculous unfold.*

*The love that most have known has been a clever imitator of the
real Love that is at the core of your Being. The love that most
have known is the love that is thought of as a commodity. This*

imposter of love brings no comfort. The love that most have known has been used to bring accommodation, not inclusion. The love that most have known has been used to represent control over another. In such ways, it has been used as follows: "I will love you when," or "I will love you if" - always with condition and terms that hold another bound.

This is not the purity of the True Love of which we speak. The Love that is your truest Power is the Love that holds no one bound. It is the Love that includes all things, all people, all beliefs and all circumstances. It is the kind of Love that creates Peace, in the truest sense, at the gateway to your heart. When this Love is known, it will never be denied.

Look within yourselves this day, indeed in this hour, and feel the Love within you that can set you free.

It will set you free from the need to judge or condemn, to make wrong or to make right. It will allow you to be your most honorable self at all times, in all situations and in all places. Silently invite this Love to Shine Its Light within you, so that you are warmed by its glow, soothed by its Peace and filled to such a degree that you know completely that there is abundance of Love available to all Souls. This Truth has always been and will forever be.

Live fully by using the Love that is your essence. It is the calling card that precedes you and the warm glow of its presence will linger after your departure from a conversation, an event and even this lifetime. Let Love be your signature, your guiding Light, your peaceful countenance and your truest Gift to all who know you in this Life and beyond."

Quantum physicists are changing the way we view our world. It's a wonderful thing. Science is, after all, studying Creation and all that has been put here for us to discover. In my view, science is the study of Creation - the study of God. Trying to separate the two is futile.

There are more things unknown to us than are known. As mysteries are being observed and investigated we are shown that we are integral parts of everything that we observe. Science has postulated that the outcome of experiments can be influenced by the expectations of the researcher. We certainly know that we have direct influence on the "placebo effect." We just don't understand how. Our beliefs and expectations directly affect outcomes. Perhaps it is time to recognize the significance of this action. We can change what we view by our response to it. Emotions ignite action. Apathy creates a standstill.

Many times we find ourselves wanting things that we do not have with the illusive thought that "something" will bring us the happiness we all crave. Far too often we fail to see that our redundant, negative thinking encapsulates us in our own mindset and we forget that we can make a change for the better by changing what we focus on.

One of the greatest human tragedies occurs when we fail to recognize that we have the power to change our own minds. We have the gift of Free Will at our disposal each and every minute of each and every day. It never goes away. It is there for us to employ, to use the Power of Choice to change everything about our lives, from the subtle to the magnificent. When we engage a Change of Heart we witness the Power inherent within that change.

Let me illustrate a common theme that I witness frequently. People believe that their stories define them. "I am this way because my mother/father was an alcoholic," or "My wife/husband cheated on me," or "I hate my boss and my finances are in ruin." Most people have experienced difficulties or have had some loss that has deeply affected them, but it is not true that the emotional signatures triggered by those events are irrevocable. Certainly events cannot be undone, but our reaction to those events is malleable and can be transformed by our understanding and a different point of view.

Understanding events, particularity when they involve other people, does not condone anyone's poor behavior. Rather, it gives us the opportunity to look through different eyes and begin to comprehend the emotional instability that unexamined reactions cause. We can easily find ourselves in emotional whirlwinds, often forgetting that we can firmly plant our feet on the ground, observe what is happening, and make a different choice.

The problem lies in what we allow to bind us, often in unhealthy ways. When relationships have eroded to abuse, regardless of what that relationship might be, we must be truthful with ourselves and recognize that Love is being denied. It is not possible for Love not to be Present, for Love is the force that animates all things. Rather it is the denial of the existence of Love that is the problem. From that denial of the Power that Love has, we blindly give ourselves permission to lash out at others instead of taking a moment for self-examination. One moment of self-reflection can help us re-discover the Love that we have denied in ourselves.

That does not mean for one second that anyone should stay in an abusive relationship. It means that we have the opportunity to feel the Power of Self-Love that can help us to see more clearly, looking truthfully at what has happened so that we can learn our own strengths.

There is great Power in a Peaceful Heart. It is the Power that can change everything and can offer us the opportunity to see the beautiful and the miraculous within ourselves. From that place of Peace we can leave behind the crippling legacy of denial of Love and employ Love's vast Power that can help us leave our wounds behind. I often tell people that they can be their own CEO, Chief Energy Operator, and in that position they can choose to build a Life fueled by Love.

YOU CREATE WITH YOUR LOVE

"Everything that irritates us
about others
can lead us to an understanding
of ourselves."

Carl Jung

Spirit Message
May 5, 2010
5:20 pm

"You are loved. You are LOVE. You were created in Love, and your very essence is Love. Can you begin to comprehend that most valuable knowledge? It is, in truth, the Key to your Happiness, the Key to your Health, the Key to your comfort and the Key to your Joy.

Love is the essence of your nature, your being and your atomic structure. Yes, your very atoms are created by Love, maintained by Love and reproduced by Love. Nothing else has that Power. Nothing else can create beauty like Love can.

Our clear vantage point allows us to witness humankind's illusions begin to fall away. In the midst of the collapse of unhealthy structures Humanity can begin the act of creation of new and sustainable ways of living.

It is by your Love that you are known and it is by your Love that you create. Do not, for one precious second of your life, neglect to hold this Truth as Sacred. You create with your Love.

If you fully understood the Power in the statement, "You create with your Love," you would recognize that you have the power to move mountains. You have the Power to end hunger and you have the Power to stop oppression in all its many ways. The illusion that you are powerless is self-limiting. Nothing will remain the same when you create with your Love. In particular, any structure that does not support the betterment of humankind will crumble because its foundation was built upon shaky ground.

As humanity begins to embrace the magnificent Power inherent in your Love, and feel and know your own connection to The Source of All Love, you will begin to change everything about your way of life. It is the dissolution of an illusion that brings clarity. So rejoice in the coming days and know that all of the things that you see failing are making way for a better, more conscious ways of being. Rejoice in knowing that Love will always prevail, so add your Love to the mix of your human experience and all will be well.

Look beyond your comfort zones and recognize how uncomfortable you have been. Create transparency in your workplace, in your homes, in your conversations, in your thoughts and in every moment. As the illusions fall away you will see what you are made of... the abounding, never ceasing, always increasing awareness of Love. And you will witness miracles every day, and embrace the blessing of the limitless Power of Love that is always and everywhere at your disposal...for it is you. You are and have always been Love that has no end."

We create unnecessary problems. Each and every one of us has. We don't like to admit it, but it is true. Each time you have done something and didn't do it to the best of your ability, you have created a problem. How many times have you done things partially, thinking that it was good enough, knowing all the while that you didn't give it your all? Then later you might wonder why you got a C instead of an A or you didn't get the promotion that you were expecting. More than likely, you didn't give it your all – and you knew it. It is funny how we try to fool ourselves and then are angered by the outcome.

It is time that we start giving our all and no longer be willing to just get by with what has been the norm, but truly give 100% or better. Can you imagine how our world would change for others and ourselves?

Humanity has been taught that we are at odds with each other, that we have to compete with one another, that it is us against them, man against woman, nation against nation, race against race. And this is simply false. We are all in this Life together, and sooner or later we have to begin to embrace this understanding.

On any given day we can listen to the radio or watch television and hear account after account of horrific events one person has perpetrated against another. This is all a choice, and that choice is the denial of Love and its importance and its Power to change everything. It is rare that a human being does not know that what they are doing is wrong, even when they espouse that their religious convictions dictate their actions.

Deep in the human heart we know right from wrong. The problem is that we confuse ideology with right conduct. We defend our need to be right and thereby abdicate our responsibility to do what is right. All the while we know that there are consequences for us when we deny Love's pure Power.

Create beauty in your thinking. Release prejudice from your mind. Cultivate generosity in thought, word and deed so that no one will be left wanting. It is up to you, it is up to me, and I believe we are up to the task.

ELAINE M. GROHMAN

truth is necessary
for peace
the heart
will never find
peace
without it

Elaine M. Grohman

ONLY YOU CAN BE YOU

"We are stardust,
we are golden,
and we've got to get ourselves
back to the garden."

Joni Mitchell

Spirit Message
Friday, May 7, 2010
8:11am

"Be yourself today. Really, be yourself today. Let your truest nature shine from you today. Smile from deep within you, and let others begin to know who you are.

Human beings pretend in the presence of others. It is not good to pretend to be anyone other than who you are. It is observed that people behave one way with one group of people, and an entirely different with another. This causes great confusion and pain within the human heart.

Do not fear judgment, for that it is the singular reason why people transform themselves on the outside to fit into particular situations. Be yourself, it is the greatest gift that you can give to the world.

When you are truly yourself the goodness and beauty that is you can shine forth. It takes great effort to try to conform to others ideals of you, and in those circumstances you will always fall short. For what one may like another may not, and that is how it is.

When you are your truest self at all times, you blossom from the inside, showing the magnificence of who you are on the outside. Then you shine your Light for all to see and know that your place in this lifetime is as important as their own. Together you will all be Lights unto the World.

Like flickering flames bring a soft glow and comfort, so too will your Light be a glow for others, allowing them to feel the Peace that enables them to be their truest selves along with you.

This Light will illuminate the Human Soul and humanity will begin to heal."

———————————

It's funny how Spirit shows me things. It happens all of the time and I really do appreciate it. Writing blocks come with the territory of being a writer and can present challenges, but thankfully it usually doesn't last long. I have found that the best thing to do is ask one simple question… "What would You like me to write about?" and invariably something happens that illuminates my thinking. I needed some time to think, to clear my mind in order to listen to Spirit guide me. I thought about doing something to relax, like getting my nails done. It is such a lovely feeling when you can close your eyes and let someone do something for you. It helps both parties.

I drove to the nail salon and saw that they had closed – permanently. The storefront was empty with no forwarding information. I half expected it to be closed as over time many of the stores in that strip mall had closed their doors. I thought of the family that had worked so tirelessly together, and what a struggle it must have been to hang on until there was nothing left to hang on to. I silently wished them well.

I realized that I was being given more time to think, to free my writer's block and perhaps learn something in the process. It is easy to get upset in those situations but I have learned to ask Spirit what I should do instead. "Go to the nail salon near your home," was the gentle nudge. "Okay," I thought, although I had never been there before.

I pulled into the parking lot and as I walked up to the entrance a beautiful Vietnamese woman smiled at me as she unlocked the door. I was the only customer. Another younger woman was there, strikingly beautiful, elegant in her movements and with a gentle smile. They were mother and daughter.

The mother began my pedicure, gently soothing my tired feet as she made casual conversation. Her daughter came over and started my manicure. Their energy was like a warm smile that welcomed me in as they carefully offered their service.

I moved to the daughter's station and our conversation deepened. "I want to thank you for being so peaceful," she said, "so many people come in here and treat us as if we are their servants. Over time I realized that I was seeing their sadness. It used to upset me, but now I just say a prayer for them. When we first opened four years ago, it seemed that so many people who came in here were not very pleasant. We just decided to be ourselves and to be kind to them. Gradually, they stopped coming in, and now we don't have as many nasty people here. It is refreshing to be able to have a warm conversation with someone."

She talked about the love she has for her family, her mother in particular, and the joy that she feels when she is able to spend time with her grandfather in Vietnam. "Whenever we visit, I make a point of getting up early in the morning to have coffee with him. He tells wonderful stories. He was there during the fall of Saigon. He helped so many people all the while being in danger himself. He is such a gentle, wise man. I wish that people would see beyond who they think we are, and know that we all are here to love and support one another."

Nothing ever happens by accident. The gift can be found if we are ourselves and recognize that we all want the same things. I was touched by her candor and grateful that Spirit had guided me there.

*when we come
together in harmony
our differences are
celebrated and
cherished*

Elaine M. Grohman

The Problem Of Judgment

"Do not look where you fell,
but where you slipped."

African Proverb

Spirit Message
May 16, 2010
10:58 am

"The first step that is necessary to bring about the solution to a problem is to ask one simple question... Is Love present here?

Throughout life you will encounter what appears to be a problem, and the human response has habitually been to try to do one of two things: fight the problem or attempt to find a solution to a problem. We, your Divine Friends, would like to suggest a third alternative. Rather than fighting or being staunch in your determination to "prove" your position as being the best, consider taking a different tract.

Look at any situation that causes disturbance and ask... "Is Love present here?"

One has an opportunity in these circumstances to take a step back and truly observe what is happening. Unfortunately judgment is often a first response. Judgment is neither accurate nor helpful. We would suggest that you hesitate for just one moment, resist the temptation to make a judgment, and simply observe what is going on before you.

As you witness an angry situation, do not judge this as bad... rather, allow yourself to see what we see... an absence of Love. The act of judgment creates immediate separation, pitting one against another, with the illusion that one is "right" and the other "wrong." Neither of these judgments will bring about a peaceful and immediate change.

Look with Loving eyes upon anything that you have judged, and ask that Love be brought to the situation. Let Love be the solution to the turmoil. Let Love be the gentle Hand that unties the knots of hatred and resentment. Judgment is the greatest tragedy that occurs within the hearts of humankind.

No longer bring judgment to any situation, rather bring aware-ness. Look with Loving Eyes so that Love can bring solutions to the struggles within the human heart. Let Love be present - al-ways and in all ways.

Whether conflict is within your heart, your home, your neighbor-hood, your community, your country or your world, see the con-flict and notice one thing... Love is not present. Through the greatest gift that you possess, your own Loving Heart, send forth the energy of Love, allowing it to emanate from your Sacred Cen-ter and reverberate through the cosmos, and invite Love to be the solution.

It is only when you look at one another with Loving Eyes that you will begin to embrace the Peace that can be your Kingdom within at any Moment. Send Love where it is denied. Be Love wherever you go, and your world, your lives and your Heart will heal and you will witness the Miracle that Love lays at your feet for you to use with open and generous abandon. "

Until we take notice of a problem nothing can be resolved. Often the problem is not "out there" but rather inside our own perspective. For a long time my perspective was skewed. Countless nights I have laid awake worrying about one thing or another and far too often my worry was followed by anger. No amount of worry on my part seemed to make much difference. Try as I might, worry brought nothing but an endless cycle of distress.

I know I am not alone in this senseless internal dialogue that is neither productive nor inspiring. At the end of the day, worry can be the singular blockage to finding a solution. I gradually began to recognize that by simply changing the words I used to identify a feeling could be empowering rather than limiting. The word "worry" implies an endless concern, seemingly without an end in sight, and can stop us in our tracks when it comes to bringing about a result that can initiate a productive change. Words can and will cause visceral reactions, literally felt in your body, and can invoke tension or calm. Choose your words wisely.

Concern, on the other hand invokes a feeling of solution, of finding a resolution to a problem. Consider taking note of the words you use to identify experiences in your life and observe what you feel inside your body. If you notice tension, reexamine your thoughts and feelings to find the cause of your distress. Try it yourself. Pay attention to the word "worry" and observe your bodily reaction. You may notice your muscles tighten, your forehead furrow, your thinking narrow. Now, think of the word "concern" and note the difference of your bodily impulse.

We often forget that words have inherent power, especially our own internal dialogue. Changing your words will open the door for Love to come into your thinking, and can broaden your worldview. Your worldview must include you, for that is where humanity will change first, within us. That Love is a vibration that allows us to look further than we have, even if that deeper view is only on the inside.

In my own mind, I have become conscious of choosing my words more carefully. Our words can empower or deflate us, and the value of that awareness is striking. Try it yourself and let Love help you dissolve worry so that a solution or acceptance can be in its place.

there is tremendous strength
in goodness
a power that needs
no force
see your own goodness
and bring it forth

Elaine M. Grohman

GOODNESS

"God enters by a private door
into every individual."

Ralph Waldo Emerson

Spirit Message
June 9, 2010
6:05 pm

"Let goodness shine forth from you today, and indeed every day
of your life. Goodness has been misunderstood for far too long.
Goodness is not weakness as some might have you believe.
Goodness is Love in Action.

When you act with goodness you begin to see the world and oth-
ers with the eyes of appreciation. Goodness is everywhere, if only
one will see. When goodness is brought to any situation, the walls
of judgment begin to tumble down and will become a mere pile
of refuse that can be swept and lifted away.

Bring goodness to your words, bring goodness to your actions,
bring goodness to your thoughts and you will discover the
strength that goodness brings. Goodness brings the freedom from
judgment. Freedom from judgment allows you to dismiss the no-
tion of superiority and brings about the peace of equality.

Today and every day bring goodness into all that you do. As you approach the end of your days you can honestly say, "I did good!"

———————————

Everyone wants goodness, but not everyone knows how to get it. Worse, they don't trust goodness when it is presented to them. It is a bit ironic, don't you think? We want it but we don't trust it. Perhaps then the problem isn't the goodness, but our lack of understanding of its implications.

Goodness, as defined by the Merriam-Webster Dictionary is: "the quality or state of being good." Goodness is synonymous with the following – character, decency, integrity and virtue. All of these can cause us to have our feet to the fire. WE have to be good in order for goodness to flourish. WE have to have decency in our thinking and actions in order for goodness to have its place in our lives. WE have to have integrity in all that we do, all that we say and all that we think if goodness is to have any chance at all.

Perhaps the real problem is our thinking. Goodness does not mean perfection – rather, it is the steadfast awareness of our actions coupled with the grace that we can employ through the vehicle of our Hearts' Loving guidance. Goodness does not mean that all the fun is taken out of life, but rather ensures that all people have the same opportunity to experience joy.

Goodness wants equality. Goodness guides with gentle hands. Goodness pauses to observe rather than judge. Goodness is our nature.

IT SHALL BE

"The whole difference between
construction and creation is exactly this:
that a thing constructed
can only be loved after it is constructed;
but a thing created is loved before it exists."

G. K. Chesterton

Spirit Message
June 17, 2010
5:22 pm

"Believe with all of your heart that goodness will be with you,
and it shall be. Believe with all of your heart that joy will be with
you, and it shall be. Believe with all of your heart that kindness
will come from you, and it shall be.

Goodness, kindness and joy are not momentary experiences.
They are a choice and a way of Being.

Let us say again, Believe with all of your Heart, and it shall be.

What you have failed to understand is that your "belief" has been
predicated on the false notion that you are not worthy. Nothing
could be further from the truth. You have had a belief that some-

thing "out there" is not on your side, and again we say nothing could be further from the truth.

Believe with all of your heart. Know now, and listen as we say... Believe WITH your heart, with your whole being, with the very essence that you are and you will be the Source of goodness. You will be the source of joy; indeed you will be the source of the kindness that you so desire.

BE it, and it is yours. Know it, and it is yours. Live it, and it is yours. It has never been withheld from you, it is only you who have withheld it from your selves and from others.

Let your Heart believe - and you will see miracles happen before you every day."

Self-doubt is perhaps one of the single most crippling problems in human evolution. We stop ourselves in countless ways, allowing self-doubt to prevent us from walking forward, from taking risks, from doing what our hearts are calling us to do.

So many times people come to me for an Angel Reading and ask, "What should I do?" The most important answer that I can ever give is not an answer at all, but rather a question. "What do you want to do?" That is what we get to ask ourselves every day. I am not talking about the little things in life, although those choices are important. I am talking about the bigger picture, the "what the heck am I here for?" kind of question.

When people honestly express their dreams they are confirming to themselves what they have longed to do. Whether that is to write a book, move to another job, start a relationship, end a relationship or open a new salon, all along they seem to know but might simply need a gentle nudge in the direction of their dreams.

One client of mine had the dream of opening a new salon. This required her to take a leap of faith. She could envision it in her mind's eye. She knew what it would look like, where it would be and what she would call it. And you know what, she did it. With a little encouragement from Spirit, she stepped confidently forward and all of the perceived obstacles fell away. Now she has a beautiful salon exactly where she had wanted. It has a warm and inviting atmosphere that is conducive to encouraging others to also follow their dreams.

This does not mean that anything you want can and should be yours. It is much too easy to become greedy and self-important. The kind of dream making that I am speaking of is belief in oneself and the abilities that can blossom within an individual, bringing one's best self to the fore. Each individual has gifts that are often hidden away, hidden by our self-doubt and fear of failure. You cannot fail to be you when you trust and believe in the longings of your heart. Ask Spirit for guidance and direction and miracles will unfold before you when you step forward in the direction of your heart's desires.

Blossom, grow, and stretch... Be You. Allow the gifts of your Life's accomplishments to encourage others to do the same with their own. You will not only lead the way, you will show the way.

CONSIDER A CHANGE OF HEART

"From a distance the earth looks blue and green
and the snow-capped mountains white.
From a distance the ocean meets the stream
and the eagle takes to flight.
From a distance there is harmony
and it echoes through the land.
It's the voice of hope.
It's the voice of peace.
It's the voice of every man."

Julie Gold

Spirit Message
July 15, 2010
8:57 am

"Consider a Change of Heart. Let us say again, consider a
change of heart. We are guardians of the Love of Creation. The
Love that heals all things, knows all things, witnesses all things
and honors all things. The Love that we speak of is everywhere
and is in every thing. From the smallest particle to the grandest
universe, there is no place where Love is absent. It can be no
other way. Love exists everywhere.

We ask that you consider a change of heart. As we stand by your
side we know and witness the isolation that is created within the

human experience. You falsely believe that circumstances are as they are, and that you have little effect in the changes that are to come.

We ask you again to consider a Change of Heart.

Look within yourself at this moment and witness the beliefs that you choose to hold dear. Some experience resentment, some experience loneliness, some experience despair... but very few experience true Joy. There is only one solution to this unnecessary dilemma - a Change of Heart.

Consider a Change of Heart. We ask that you let your experience of loneliness fall away and know that you are never alone. Let your experience of despair fall away and know that your next choice could change your life. Let your experience of resentment fall away and feel the freedom of release from the prison you have created.

The blessing of a Change of Heart will come in the blink of an eye when you recognize, without a critical mind, the energy of these emotions that you have held close. They do not serve your continued growth, they do not promote Joy and they do not enrich your Life. Consider a Change of Heart. You have the Power of Choice.

At this moment forgive yourself for keeping Love away. Forgive yourself for not allowing your true words to come forth. Let your heart welcome joy so that you can see and feel the LOVE that surrounds you, supports you, and indeed IS YOU.

Consider a Change of Heart so that the Love of God shines from you, to you and through you.

The Love of God is the spark that beats your heart, which animates your physical being and brings each and every lesson your way. View Life with a Changed Heart and you will see the miracles that God has placed at your feet each and every day, and indeed with every step you take. Consider a Change of Heart... it will Change Everything."

You create your world through your thoughts, words and actions. There is no way of getting around it. You are totally and completely responsible for your way of being in the world and the way you react to it. Humanity is in the midst of an enormous shift in our collective thinking and we can no longer afford to deny our personal responsibility to our families, our friends, to the world and most importantly, to ourselves. Our lives are perilously short and acidic thoughts and words can kill as swiftly and as surely as the worst natural disasters.

Each and every day we are faced with choices. Each and every day you are given the opportunity to create change, often in an instance, based upon the choices that you make. Anger and the persistent feelings of resentment are not our birthright. Invariably, the abdication of responsible thinking and speech will initiate the erosion of one's own consciousness, and therefore, behavior. Left unchecked, internal, unresolved conflict will spill out and will affect external factors, including people.

You have heard the phrase, "You are what you eat." Another, perhaps more poignant phrase is, "You are what you think." Thinking is under your control. It is a conscious, intentional act that is not under the whim of some unseen influence, unless of course, mental health issues are in play. Thinking, and then by direct correlation, speaking and acting, are under your own control. Many people make excuses for their behavior and thus their thinking, without taking any responsibility for their actions or any inevitable outcomes.

Let's take a look at abuse - verbal abuse in particular. Verbal abuse is insidious, and has a cumulative effect on the abused. The use of constant degrading, undermining rhetoric will most definitely affect the one to whom the words are directed, but without a doubt, the one who initiates the detrimental language is causing untold harm to himself/herself. No one can truthfully abdicate his or her responsibility for right behavior, saying that he or she does not know any better for Creation will not allow this denial to go on indefinitely. Often, the abusive individual will cloak their true selves when in the presence of others. Still, Spirit always knows what is going on, and the karmic impact of selective amnesia nonetheless will leave a karmic debt that will need correction. It is only a matter of Time.

The roar of unkindness will shake humanity to its core if it is left unchecked. Those who have been courageous and driven by Love are able to walk away from abuse, in any form, with heads held high and hearts wide open. Walking away from abuse can initiate a change. Abuse can no longer be tolerated if we are to grow as human beings. We are capable of so much more.

Walking away from abuse does not mean that one is weak, but rather that one is strong. Love guides us toward our basic human right of self-care and self-preservation. Anger is not the absence of Love; rather, it is the denial of Love. Do not deny Love, for it is your birthright and your reason for existence. Let Love be what you seek, and never confuse love with control. Love never controls. Love releases each of us to be our truest selves and allows us to release unkindness in our wake, and welcomes true Love to blossom before us, around us and within us.

there is harmony
in everything
that exists
a delicate balance
that can bring
all of existence
back to its center
to the point
of stillness
where harmony
resides

Elaine M. Grohman

YOUR WORLD

"The noblest service
comes from nameless hands.
And the best servant
does his work unseen."

Oliver Wendall Holmes

Spirit Message
August 4, 2010
4:31 pm

"Have you ever considered that your thoughts reverberate across
the Cosmos? Have you ever imagined that your thoughts move
through time and space and affect all that they encounter?

Please know, dear ones, that your thoughts create your reality
and that your reality is created by your thoughts. There is an in-
termingling of energies and therefore a direct correlation between
the quality of your thoughts and the quality of your experience
called Life.

Be ever aware that goodness and kindness are the hallmark of
loving thoughts. Even in the midst of difficulty, begin with kind
thoughts and you will send kindness into the ethers. The scope
of your reach is staggering; the breadth of your influence is be-

yond measure.

Let your thoughts steer towards healing and may your mind rest quietly so that solutions can be found to problems that you encounter. Be grateful and be at peace. It is your world; direct it with your Love."

Sitting at my computer in the late evening I appreciated the silence that enfolded me. I have just asked Spirit what I should write. The light of the computer screen illuminated the room with a soft glow and I closed my eyes to listen like a patient fisherman. The soft silence was broken by a rhythmic sound outside. It startled me at first and I could hardly believe what I was hearing.

The sound felt directed to me, as if a past memory had flashed through my mind, reminding me that Nature is our loving guide as well as our treasured home. This time, the sounds seems like it was just outside my window. "Whoo, whooo." I listened to the gentle invitation to come outside. Stepping outdoors, my feet broke through the thin layer of crusted snow. The cold, crisp air alerted my senses as I entered the private domain of the nocturnal world.

The night enveloped me as I stood silently - listening. "Whoo, whooo," seemed louder than before and I half expected this illusive creature to be sitting on the rocks outside my door. I wandered and wondered as the gentle voice guided me through the darkness. Following the sound past the massive stone walls behind our home, it seemed as though these ancient stone guardians of time amplified the magical voice of this winged guest. I followed.

My eyes adjusted to the deep veil of night and I continued to walk toward the hill behind our home. And still, the voice called me to come further. Suddenly, I saw him, high in the branches of the leaf barren poplar tree that stands like a sentinel on the top of the hill guarding this land. And he called me yet again.

I could see his silhouette against the drape of sky and he turned his head, as only an owl can, to confirm my wonder as to the identity of this Magical Brother. "Whoo, whooo," he called to me again. The wonderful sound caused goose bumps on my flesh as the acoustics of Nature moved his voice all around me. I dared to speak, attempting in my foreign tongue to tell him that I had heard his call. Suddenly, my eyes saw movement several branches above and I could hardly believe what I was seeing. Not one, but two owls were calling to me in the night.

Silent tears filled my eyes as my heart swelled with gratitude for this interaction between the three of us. Only our voices could be heard. We began a conversation, as I clumsily introduced myself to these visitors who had graced me with their company. "Whoo, whooo," I echoed in their direction, in my distinct human dialect. They turned their heads to look at the creature below them who was clumsily endeavoring to communicate. They replied to me and I was struck by the magic of that moment. They knew that I am not as comfortable in the darkness as they were and they gently offered their guidance and wisdom to me in their own language. Somehow, I understood.

These two friends had shown me the importance of asking for assistance, and then silencing the mind long enough to hear the reply. Like those winged friends, our fellow travelers in Life, our brothers and sisters in this tribe of humanity, call for our attention, both quietly and boisterously, seeking our assistance, our acceptance, our understanding – our Love. For it is Our World, Our Lives that cry for us, silently awaiting our reply.

YOU ARE THE GARDENER

"The gardener sows seeds
with love and care, to ensure that Life
will continue there."

Elaine M. Grohman 1986

Spirit Message
August 18, 2010
5:30 pm

"It is time to tend to your own garden. Clean up the debris. Cut
away what is dead and is no longer blossoming. Let new life
begin to emerge from the clutter.

It is time to clean up your own back yard. Brush away the debris,
remove any unwanted materials, gift to others those things that
you no longer use or need. Clean up your own back yard.

It is time to look within you. Be willing to release the old wounds
that you have allowed to become your story. Forgive them now.
Allow the debris of anger to be collected and released from your
life; allow the clean fresh air of Love to be what you focus upon
now.

It is time to look around your neighborhood. Who do you really know? How have you made judgments of others? No longer have your perceptions direct your heart, but rather let your humanity shine from you to share your Light with others.

As you tend to your own garden, to your own back yard, to your own heart, you will see that there is much work to be done - here in this Lifetime.

Begin without hesitation, and the grandeur of this life will shine forth for you. You will see it gleaming from the eyes of those around you. You will feel it as you look at the beauty of one's life being tended to. When all of the debris is taken away, you will see the fullness of the gifts that Life has to offer.

Clean up your home, your precious Mother Earth, so that others may truly live."

I had neglected my garden for some time. Sure, it was beautiful, but I knew what needed to be done and how much more beautiful it could be. But I was tired, and the job seemed overwhelming. But I walked into the garage to get my tools and looked at the splendor that surrounded me. Before I could think, my mind flashed back to the time when there wasn't a single flower to be seen. Now our home is surrounded by gardens and ever-changing beauty. I felt overwhelmed by the sheer amount of work to be done. Nevertheless, I took out my hand sheers and began to trim. "Where should I begin?" I asked. "It doesn't matter, just begin."

As I worked in the garden, the warmth of the sun relaxed my muscles and then my mind, as I rhythmically moved from one area to another. Stepping into the soft soil my foot sank slightly and I was struck by the notion that this good, rich Earth had provided so much. All it needed was my attention and willingness to simply begin. The hours drifted by and before long I stood looking at the fruits of my efforts. The garden needed me as much as I needed it, and before long, with refreshing sweat on my forehead I paused and smiled.

At times we convince ourselves that we are stuck. That the situations we find ourselves in are insurmountable, unmanageable and therefore we are unable to move beyond the problem. Many believe this illusion since we are often taught that there is only so much to go around. Invariably this causes anger and clouded thinking.

We have many ways to get out of our self-imposed limitations and usually the solutions are not as difficult as we often believe. The single obstacle that gets in our way is that we simply do not ask. "Ask and you shall receive," is a very powerful statement, perhaps the most Powerful statement we can engage.

Recently I had a conversation with someone who believed that things were tough, and that the situation he found himself in was impossible to resolve. "How often do you ask Creation for help?" I asked. He looked puzzled, as though I had just asked him to jump off a bridge. "How do I ask?" he inquired.

Time and time again, Spirit has shown that our thinking is limited by our belief that there is not enough, or worse, that we are not deserving. But the truth is that we all deserve happiness, joy and prosperity but we either don't know what to do or we don't believe in our own abilities to begin, and then we are stuck.

I reminded this young man about the dreams he had shared with me regarding using his talents and God given gifts to be helpful to others. Unfortunately, many people believe if they fervently ask for something, that they will receive their hearts' desires. What we have failed to recognize is that WE have to begin to walk in the direction of our dreams so that Creation knows that we really mean it. Beginning is half the battle.

Discarding old ways, old beliefs and unhealthy thinking will help you to perceive. Someone who wants to be an author needs to begin to write. Someone who wants to be a famous photographer has to begin to take photos. One thing leads to another, and our belief in ourselves will grow as we begin.

If you want a beautiful garden you have to tend to it. Cutting away that which is spent to make way for new growth is essential. It is the act of trimming, watering, grooming and blessing that the garden will show the bounty of your efforts. Your life is the same. Begin today to quiet the doubts within you by stepping toward your goals. It is not the destination but the journey that brings about the bounty. If something doesn't work, give thanks for what you have learned and try something new in its place.

Like a gardener, you must first prepare the soil, your own heart, and then plant the seeds of your desires and tend to them with care and steadfastness. As the seasons change you will look back at all of the steps that helped you to get to your destination, where you can take yet another step as you expand the variety of experiences you wish to enjoy. Ask, and then move in that direction, and the Universe will surprise and delight you every day.

A GUIDING LIGHT

*"Man's main task in life is to give birth to himself,
to become who he potentially is.
The most important product of his effort
is his own personality."*

Erich Fromm

Spirit Message
September 16, 2010
3:45 pm

*"The Human Race is in the midst of a great awakening. This
awakening has always been available to all peoples at all times
in history.*

*Yet now is the only time that matters. The great awakening is the
Gift of Awareness of the Preciousness of this Life. YOUR Life.*

*Most people run from experiencing life and instead allow labels
and conformity to thwart their experience of knowing who they
really are. You are not the label that has been given to you. You
are not simply your gender, your race, your age and your profes-
sion. You are a Being whose purpose is to experience and express
the Love that you are.*

Sometimes we see that you are confronted with challenges, and rather than meet and overcome the challenge you find yourself falling into the trap of labeling yourself, and thus allowing disillusionment to have greater control of your will to experience Life.

Challenge yourself at this time to allow your illusions of yourself to fall away. You cannot know the greatness that your Life presents to you until you step away from your limiting views.

If it is anger that is your constant companion, do not let anger be your deterrent, let the fire of anger smolder and be a constant heat that ignites your passion. If lack of self-belief is halting you, see the beauty around you, thus allowing you to begin to believe in the goodness within you, and the millions upon millions of opportunities that opened to you within your lifetime will be seen, known and available.

The greatest experience that a Human Being can strive for is Love. Love of self is a Power that brings all of your goodness, all of your gifts, both the hidden and the known, into play in your decision-making. Let the Fire of Love ignite your heart, ignite your Mind and infuse your Spirit with the Energy that brings its intensity to burn away your labels and Light your way to the realities you wish to express.

In so doing, you will be the Fire, truly, the Light for others to see. Let the Flame of Love burn brightly within you, and let illusions be seen for what they are. Shadows will lose their potency when Light is shone upon them. Let the shadows of your labels be brought to the Light of Day, the Light of the pure expression of Love that you are.

Put no faith in the power of illusions, the limitations of labels, of yourself or others, and bring forth all illusions into the Light.

Then and there you will see that Love is the Guiding Light, the Healing Balm, the Tender Caress that allows you to see your true potential as a Human Being.

Express that Love today. Believe in yourself, Today. Let Love be your signature - Today. Begin to truly live... TODAY."

Through numerous readings, I have experienced the vibrations of those who have taken their own lives. There is a palpable regret that I notice, which is sad but not frightening.

Whether directly or indirectly, death can come before its appointed time, in the form of suicide or self-destructive behavior. There are many ways to kill your spirit, but there is only one cause - the lack of Love for oneself. Through the help of Spirit, these souls have a sense of clarity for their actions that culminated in their death.

Without exception, Spirit is present, acting as gentle guides who help to amplify the human vibration so that a message can be given. Spirit stands side by side with the individual as trusted Truth-Bearers, ensuring that all parties will share Truth. There is a sense of remorse and responsibility that cannot be denied. Inevitably, tears begin to flow as the deceased asks for forgiveness.

I have come to understand that there is always great compassion for the person who does not know how to live in this world and thereby ends their life prematurely. When individuals believe in limitations, brought about by self and/or other imposed labels, we all lose. We cannot shy from our responsibility to treat one another with kindness, for we do not know the wounds that others bear.

There are people that I know who have committed suicide and the one, common factor that weaves through their lives is that they believed that life was not fair to them and their thinking became an endless loop of anger, mistrust or need for validation. The first time I had this experience I was nineteen years old.

I started working at a pharmacy when I was fifteen years old. My older sister, Dianne, was working at a local pediatric office and heard that the pharmacist in the adjoining building needed some part-time help. I would go to work immediately after school from 2:30 pm until 6:00 pm each weekday and 9:00 am to 6:00 pm each Saturday.

There was one gentleman who came in once or twice a week, mostly to visit. John was a quiet man, perhaps in his early sixties. He had never married and lived his whole life taking care of his mother. At times they seemed to have a peaceful relationship, while at other times he would comment about his life being so consumed with her care and demands that he had not been able to live his own. He had hoped to be married and have his own family, but it was not to be. Having experienced the deaths of both my brother and my mother at twelve and thirteen years old respectfully, there was a sadness about him that resonated with my own. I didn't quite understand it at the time.

He had a strong sense of responsibility, which at times became burdensome and was often palpable just below the surface. It was uncomfortable to be near him during those times but he would come in to talk to my boss, and he always seemed a bit brighter when he left. The one thing that was distinctly his own was his great love for nature and photography, and he was very good at it. He was very particular and wanted everything to be "right," and if things weren't perfect he would do them again.

I continued to work at the pharmacy after high school graduation and into college where I was taking liberal arts classes at the local community college. I had an art class and John was always delighted to hear about my latest projects. Before the end of the semester, my art instructor had encouraged me to put together a portfolio and apply to the Center for Creative Studies – The College of Art and Design.

I was accepted. I knew that I would not be able to continue working and carry a full eighteen-credit load. As my time at the pharmacy began to dwindle, John started coming in every day, bringing his latest photos. He would ask for my opinions and if I made one suggestion, he would go out that day and reshoot the photos and bring the prints in for me to see. I was in no position to be a photographic critic and I told him so, but his urgency for validation was spiraling out of control.

I soon learned that his mother had died and his sister wanted to sell the only home he had ever known. In his words, "She feels entitled to sell the home in order to get her inheritance." His anger at having "sacrificed" his life for his mother was constantly spilling over. I tried to encourage him but it was far beyond my scope of abilities. My last day of work had arrived and John came in with a small box wrapped with a ribbon. Inside was my favorite delicacy, a napoleon pastry, which he had brought in each year on my birthday. He told me that my life was blossoming and that it was like a birthday for me. I thanked him for his friendship and encouraged him to continue his beautiful photography. My career at the pharmacy was over.

I didn't go back to the pharmacy for a long time. So much time had been spent there and I enjoyed the taste of freedom from working six days a week for the past four years. Creating artwork brought me back into a world of deep meditative states, although at the time I would not have called it meditation. Every now and then John would pop into my mind. It often puzzled me and I had the strangest feeling that he wanted me to know he was okay. In fact, one time his face came so vividly to me that I was startled, and I heard his distinct voice say, "Thank you for your friendship, it meant more to me than you know." I wondered why I heard the word "meant." I let it go.

One day I was driving near the pharmacy and decided to stop in to say hello to my former boss. He greeted me warmly and after a time I asked him how John was doing. He became quiet, and then began to speak. "Elaine, I didn't want to tell you, and in fact I know that he did not want you to know until after the fact. John committed suicide." I felt a stab in my heart, and a sense that somehow I knew this might happen.

"John was distraught over the sale of the house, and he felt that he was being pushed out of his home. His sister, however, felt entitled to her half of the estate, even though she rarely assisted with their mother's care. John felt that if he couldn't have it, no one should.

He was meticulous about the care of the home and always had been. He cleaned the house from top to bottom, and then closed all of the windows. He soaked cloths in kerosene and started a fire. He was found in the clean bathtub, with his head facing the drain and a towel folded neatly under his head. John shot himself. He died instantly." My heart stopped and tears rolled down my face. It became clear to me why John had come to mind, and now I knew that it wasn't my imagination. I immediately prayed for him, hoping that he truly had found some peace and that he knew that he was a good man.

He was so meticulous that he put his best suit, shirt and his favorite tie in a box on the back porch, along with a note expressing his thoughts and feelings. He felt he had given his all and that life had given nothing back. His hope had been to destroy the home, saying that if he could not have the home then no one would. What he did not anticipate was that he had closed the house up so tight that the flames died out for lack of oxygen. Or perhaps, Spirit intervened.

We must pay closer attention to ourselves and others and the feelings that limit self-understanding. John was a good man who offered to share the beauty that he saw through his camera lens. The problem was that he couldn't see the beauty within himself. It was tragic.

Many years later a friend bought the home immediately next door to John's home. A happy young family was living there, and each time I visited my friend I thought of John and hoped that he knew how important his life was. Now, through the work that I do, I see the ramification of a life intentionally cut short. Life is a journey that is meant to be lived. Make your life count, and if you know others who have forgotten the importance of their own, please, take their hand and help them to see if you can. It is not your responsibility, but it is your opportunity.

THE ILLUSION OF LIMITATION

*"We are wide-eyed in contemplating the possibility
that life may exist elsewhere in the universe,
but we wear blinders when contemplating
the possibilities of life on earth."*

Christopher Isherwood

Spirit Message
September 17, 2010
11:34 am

"Within the confines of human consciousness there lies a great reservoir of knowledge that as yet has gone untapped. Humanity has allowed itself to be trapped in limited thinking. Some adventurous souls however, have been wise enough to give little credence to their known perspectives in order to look beyond the horizon to the vastness that lies beyond sight.

It is the purpose of your life to become an adventurer. To step away from the limitations of what appears to be known so that you can begin to forge new ground. In so doing, you will begin to free your mind and your heart from the burdens that you have held as your truth.

Your Life is meant to be an adventure into exploring the Wonders of Creation, the Beauty of Nature and, most importantly the Treasures that lie within your own hearts. You cannot fail in the role of adventurer, for it is in the exploration of your capabilities that you can begin to see the wonder of you, that we, your ever present friends and companions, can clearly see within you. You have allowed yourselves to become fearful of Change, yet it is through Change that you begin to know who you are.

Look with wonder at the people around you. Look with tenderness on the situations that appear to be limited and bless them with your Love, so that you and others will begin to know that limitations are false. Do not believe the limited thinking that you are right or that you are wrong, for you will always be standing on the brink of wonder if you choose to limit your perceptions. There is no right or wrong, there are merely perceptions that do or do not serve humanity. Begin to serve humanity and you will serve your own Life as well. Begin to serve others with your kind words, kind works and kind thoughts.

Do not judge, but rather, guide, with your Heart. Let the Adventure Begin."

I have a friend who is truly an inspiration. She is an adventurer - with sparkles. In fact, our group of friends lovingly calls her "Shishi Mama," partly because she is always impeccably dressed but mostly because she simply sparkles with enthusiasm for life. To put it simply, she is fancy. Her name is Karen.

A number of years ago she made the decision to move to New York. She packed her belongings and drove with her father to

New York City. She relished city life and whenever she had visitors you would have thought that she was the mayor, rolling out the red carpet and ensuring that everyone had a wonderful time.

Karen's dearest childhood friend, Kat, also a treasured friend of mine, invited me to go with her to visit Karen in New York. Karen graciously offered to arrange for me to see some of her friends and acquaintances while I was there. After seeing clients, she made sure that we took advantage of every waking moment. We walked, we took cabs, we rode the subway, and we even went to a Broadway show, all under Karen's watchful, loving eyes.

In February 2007, after several years in the big city, she "knew" that it was time to leave. Her treasured boss was retiring, her lease was coming to an end and she knew that it was time to go. She had done all that she wanted to do in New York and now she set her sites on her next big adventure. This time Karen's destination was Los Angeles.

She loved Kat's baby blue BMW and asked if she could buy it knowing that her lease was up. She needed a car since she hadn't had one in New York and after all, a "Shishi Mama" loves to arrive in style. It wasn't that she was showy, far from it; she loved that car and knew that it would make her happy to drive it. They were able to work out the arrangements and soon Kat and Karen made the long trip across the country to LA.

There was plenty of time for laughter, reminiscing and sharing hopes, dreams and intentions. Kat suggested they stop in Sedona so that they could spend some time at Cathedral Rock. Cathedral Rock is an awesome sight to see, its blazing red rock gleams in the sun, projecting power to all who view Her.

Kat told Karen, "When we get to Cathedral Rock, say your intentions out loud so the Universe can hear your thoughts, and then, just let it go." Once they arrived they decided to spend some quite time alone to communicate their intentions to Creation. They did not share their thoughts at that time, but simply honored the intentions of the other, as only dear friends would. After leaving Cathedral Rock, Karen decided to buy two bottles of wine. One bottle was enjoyed that evening while the other bottle was tucked away. Karen said, "One day, we will have this bottle in commemoration of this event."

Arriving in Los Angeles they quickly were able to find her apartment and get Karen settled in before Kat returned home to Michigan. In short order Karen found a job, and in August 2007, she met Deano, the man of her dreams, in a spinning class. It was only then that Karen shared her intentions with Kat that she had spoken to the Universe months ago at Cathedral Rock. "Kat, I want to tell you what I said that day in Sedona. I told Creation that my purpose in moving to California was to start a new life, find a great job, one in which I would not have to work my life away, and most importantly, to meet my life's partner, someone with mutual goals and dreams who possessed the qualities of my most favorite people - the chivalry of both my father and brother and all the best qualities of my girlfriends. I envisioned my wedding ceremony taking place at the ocean, in a beautiful location with loved ones in attendance."

Creation was listening. Karen and Deano fell in love and on November 12, 2007, the anniversary of Kat's precious mother's death, Deano asked Karen to marry him. On July 24, 2008, they were married at the Ritz Carlton, overlooking the ocean, just as Karen had envisioned. Kat has a photo of Karen, Deano and herself drinking that second bottle of wine and in that photo several

Spirit orbs reveal their loving support.

Karen followed her heart and all that she had hoped for became her new life. Now, Karen and her wonderful husband Deano, not only share their love but they also share their enthusiasm for life by helping others to find their dreams. Both Karen and Deano are joyful adventurers on this wonderful journey called Life.

Deano later shared with Karen that he too had been speaking to Creation. In August 2007, while traveling through a powerful vortex in California, he asked Spirit to help him find his soul mate. Two people, in two separate power places, were speaking to Spirit about the same desire at the same time. Call it luck, call it amazing or call it Love. It is all the same anyways.

Trust Creation, open your heart, and enjoy the ride, even if you don't have a pretty, baby blue Beemer.

do not be fooled
by the tumblers of time
the only time
that has any importance
is the ever present now
be present in your life
at this precious moment
and all of the sorrows of
the past will become
like blessed steps
that brought you to this
moment, now

Elaine M. Grohman

LOVE, SPIRIT AND CHANGE

*"How could there be any question
of acquiring or possessing,
when the one thing needful for a man
is to become -
to be at last, and to die in the fullness
of his being."*

Antoine de Saint-Exupery

Spirit Message
October 9, 2010
12:18 pm

*"We, your Angelic partners, see you ever seeking for the gift that
will change your life. We wish for you to know this day that YOU
are the gift.*

*You are the gift that can be brought forth at any time, to any place
and to any circumstance. No longer look outside of yourselves
for the answer that will bring you peace of mind.*

*Find it, where it has always been - Within you. This awareness
may bring you frustration, and that is only because you know,
deep within yourselves, that this is so. The holiness of your life
has eluded you, but know it is time to stand fully aware of the Gift
this Life brings.*

The gift that you seek is peace of mind, peace of heart and peace in your surroundings. It can never be found outside of yourself. It lies within the beauty of your Heart, within the Peace of your Soul and within the Presence that you bring.

Peace of mind begins in your own mind. Peace of Heart begins within your own heart. Peace in your surroundings is always just a change of heart away.

Look lovingly upon your own life, and know that the greatest power that has ever existed is the power of Love. Please begin today to know that you are Love. You are made from Love, you live within the Love of God and your gift is to bring that Love forth. Peace begins at that precious moment of awareness. Walk in awareness and the Beauty and Love that is your very essence will change everything in the blink of an eye. Be aware of the Holy Trinity. It consists of Love, Spirit and Change... Begin today."

My father was declining, his health increasingly fragile and his temper short. He had never been one to take direction; he was the one usually giving direction. More accurately, being the retired executive, he taught us to anticipate a need so as to prevent conflict. But, I loved this grabby character even though he had never been particularly gregarious throughout my life. My stepmother was also declining, and the two could be a challenging pair when they were on edge. Both in their eighties, they had fought to stay independent and live in their own home. In order to help that wish be fulfilled, my siblings and I took turns bringing dinner to their home each night and helping them with their nightly routine.

Thursday was my night, and on this particular evening it seemed as though I had walked into a hornet's nest. Both were cranky, feeling the drain of endless doctor visits and old, painful bodies. The tension was high. I have never done well with unnecessary confrontation. It was foreign to me. I have always preferred to be reasonable and attempt to work toward peaceful resolutions. No such luck that night.

Growing up under the watchful, loving eye of our mother, it was rare for there to be tension in our house. Aside from the occasional sibling tussle, it was a peaceful place to be. Mom was the stable force of order and guidance, direction and laughter, love and comfort. She never wavered from her position as CEO of the Hughes household, but she also never let you forget how much you were loved.

All of that changed on June 3, 1968 when our brother Brian died from Muscular Dystrophy at the tender age of fifteen. Fourteen short months later, on August 29, 1969 our Mom's life came to an untimely end, and at thirteen, my life would never be the same. Our peace was gone. Our structure was gone. Our precious mother was gone. Forever and always is a very long time.

My father, the formal executive, was left with eight surviving children, four of whom still lived at home. We managed with the loving support of older siblings and extended family but the gaping hole left by my mother's death was very deep and wide. There were times I was afraid I would drown in my sorrow if I let my tears begin to flow. Peace was our mother's trademark, and I wanted it to be mine as well.

When I was sixteen our father remarried a widow with seven children. The dramatic contrast was shocking at first, as my own heart tried to reconcile the drastic difference in personalities between our mother and our new stepmother. They could not have been more different. I knew little of romantic love and even less about the loss of a spouse so I simply tried to understand. Sometimes, I failed miserably.

Jane was also an executive, with a demanding career in the Catholic Church. She had been very accustomed to having things her way and I often found myself silent, not knowing where I fit in and attempting to help to keep the peace, unsure of how to deal with the battlefield of uncertainty my life had become.

We finally all lived together under one roof when I was seventeen. There was often tension as it was hard to know my place in the mass of humanity within their home. I never liked tension, so I would find a way to leave. I finally left when I was twenty-three when I married and started my own home and family.

But now, many year later, I was here in their home attempting to help in anyway that I could but the tension that night brought back a flood of emotions that I knew was about to boil over. After dinner, cleaning up and making sure that they were settled for the night I made an excuse to leave early rather than to watch television. Their anger was toxic that night and I could not hold it in any longer.

Funny, how Spirit can preempt an event, seemingly preparing you for something long before you have any idea what is happening. A couple of weeks before that night I had given a talk about Energy Healing at a local community center. Moments before I began the lecture, I rushed to the restroom and stopped short just before opening the door. There, immediately beside the bathroom door, was a framed map of ancient Indian trails, superimposed over a current area map of land and roads. It just so happened that one of those trails went right through our back yard. Also, oddly enough, I had just gone to a one-day workshop about Shamanism in which we would be able to learn of our "Power Animals," those precious Spirits that help us deal with life's challenges. I learned that I had two, a wolf and a black stallion.

As I politely took my leave that night I could feel the tears well up inside, fighting me as I tried to push them down. Arriving back at home I brought the baking dishes into the house and my son, Brian, was standing at the kitchen sink. He turned around and said, "What's wrong, Mama?" I tried to remain calm, placing the dishes in the sink I said, "Nothing honey, I just need to go outside for awhile." The shade of the coming dusk was comforting as it hid my emotions.

As I walked up the hill toward the back of the property my tears slowly began to flow from my eyes. I pleaded out loud to whoever was listening. "Keepers of the Land, if you are really here, I need your help right now. I can no longer hold this pain inside my heart. Please, help me to release it."

I walked toward the pond and sat on the top of the picnic table. With my feet on the bench below, I rested my head in my hands and began to cry. Suddenly I began to hear a strange sound coming from the right. "Clink, clink, clink..." I couldn't place the sound as my attention was drawn to the right. Through the veil of fading light, a single white object appeared, its rhythmic movement coming closer and closer to me. My focus fixed on a large white husky which looked very much like a wolf as it came trotting towards me. I froze, half with fear - half with wonder.

Before me stood an enormous white dog, his fur so bright it

seemed to glow in the night. He placed his two front paws between my feet on the bench and leaned towards me. Without a sound, he jumped up onto the tabletop and placed his cool, wet nose on my right cheek, just like a gentle kiss. I was frozen still, transfixed by what was happening before me.

Slowly I turned to face him and asked out loud, "Who are you?" He didn't move as we stared into each other's eyes. I felt a sudden washing away of sadness and pain, without the gripping anguish that I was afraid would crush me. It simply left. I continued to look into the eyes of this magical creature and said, "Thank you, my friend." He swiftly turned and jumped off the table and back toward the direction from which he came. I had never seen that dog before that night, and I have never seen him since.

Finally, I realized that the peace I was seeking was inside me all along. And the fear of my crushing grief gained its strength as I fought to control it. Let your feelings flow, so that Peace may come from your Heart and never be allowed to hold you captive again.

*we can be nowhere else
but in the trinity of our
own sacred selves
body, mind and spirit.
it is in this
recognition that
we see our
wholeness*

Elaine M. Grohman

ILLUMINATE YOUR WORLD

"Not what we give,
but what we share,
for the gift without the giver
is bare."

James Russell Lowell

Spirit Message
November 4, 2010
3:21 pm

"May your heart be open this evening, as the gift of Love and Awareness is shared with you. Humanity is in the midst of a most amazing time, a time in which you will have the opportunity to see yourselves, as you truly are - Beings of Love and Light. Yes, it is true; you are a Being of Love and Light. We too, your Angelic companions are often referred to as Beings of Light, and that is a truthful description. Yet, to be a Being of Light is far greater than the mere illumination that can be seen or even imagined.

The illumination that you see within us is also within you. Truly the Light that emanates from us also emanates from you, because we are one in the same, made from the same Light. Each and every human being is made of this Divine Love, the Light of Creation, and the Light of Illumination.

Your denial of this Truth has caused much unnecessary strife and pain in the human heart and in the human experience. If you were to consider, and truly take within your hearts the knowledge of the Light that is within you, you would begin to light the way for others and yourselves so that you may be guided into the Boundless Space of Love.

As humanity is presented with this great gift of awareness, know that it has never been hidden from you. It is humanity's striving for identification of being one way or another that has caused you to look everywhere but within yourselves for the answer to your perceived dilemma. In truth, all it takes is a mere change of heart and all of the chaos ceases to have validity and ceases to cause you distress. In fact, it ceases to exist at all.

We stand ever by your side, Lighting your way, so that when you see your own Light you will be able to see that same Light within your fellow human companions.

With Love we Honor you. With Light and with Gratitude we see who you truly are - Beings of Light and Love."

It is truly amazing how many people can see energy. Yes, you read that right; there are many, many people who are able to see energy - with their eyes wide open. I often tell people that if they can see a rainbow they can see energy. It is the same frequency of light. It is visible, it is measurable and it is beautiful.

Energy is visible and can be perceived as heat waves or as a soft glow, often first seen around an individual's head and shoulders. As your perception expands it is very common to see this Light fully around a person's body. All living things have dynamic energy, due to the biological activity that is maintaining life. Yet all things both animate and inanimate, have energy fields, since everything is made of atoms, and atoms are energy in action.

Growing up as an artist, I learned to be an observer. However, most people look but do not see. That is the problem. We tend to view the world through the veil of our emotions and as a consequence we see the world through our lenses of anger, fear or mistrust. Conversely, if we are fortunate, we could be blessed to see the world through the eyes of compassion, peace and our mutual humanity.

Our selective vision is a learned response. Religious, educational, cultural and family experiences often restrain our understanding of ourselves as well as our appreciation of this beautiful Mother Earth that surrounds and supports us. Many of us have walked through life with a blindfold on. We limit our experiences when we hold tight to our narrow, learned perspectives.

The human body is a resonating device, an instrument of perception, that when used more fully, can broaden our understanding of the world around us. Through focused use of our senses we can learn to see with clearer vision. Looking through the Eyes of Wonder we can begin to appreciate things in a new light, and in so doing, broaden our understanding of others and ourselves.

When we learn to abandon our prejudices and rigid thinking, we begin to make observations rather than judgments, we see with new eyes and hear with new ears. Through the gentle nudge of our senses we will begin to see all that the Earth represents and the bounty that She shares with all of us. Our lives will change when we allow Light to flow. That Light is Love in Action.

Silence Within

*"I am the maker of my own fortune.
I think of the Great Spirit
that rules this universe."*

Chief Tecumseh

Spirit Message
November 7, 2010
10:27 am

"Sit for a moment, and feel the Silence within. Feel the wonder of this quiet blessing as it offers your Soul the chance to breathe in the wonder of this experience called Life.

Sit for a moment and recall the magical fragrance of a rose. Bring its essence into you as you sit in the Silence of your own Being.

Sit for a moment and recall the fragrance of the sweet breath of an infant. Fresh and precious is that breath which brings Life into this blessed being.

Sit for a moment and recall the taste and aroma of a delicious strawberry, fresh from the vine and full of Life, willingly giving its own so that your Life may thrive.

Sit for a moment and feel the Silence within. Witness a Lifetime in a moment and bring the treasures of all of your human experiences gently into your open Heart.

Sit for a Moment. Sit for a Moment. Let this Moment awaken you to the preciousness of the stillness between each breath, between each blink of your eyes and between each and every beat of your Heart.

Sit for a Moment and know that this Gift, your Life, will never be lived again, but the treasures of the memories of all of your moments are there to be rejoiced and recounted with the ever-knowing blessing that your Life is Sacred.

Sit for a Moment and know the might that is available to your willing heart, to your willing mind and to your blessed experiences.

Sit for a Moment... and Live Fully in its Wonder."

Many of us let Life pass us by. Life is for learning and unfortunately, many times foolishness stops learning in its tracks. The greatest gift that we can receive is wisdom, but wisdom is not the same as knowledge. Knowledge needs to be acquired before wisdom can be gleaned. Wisdom is acquired once an individual has absorbed the knowledge and then knows what to do with it. Wisdom takes discernment, a synthesizing of the body of knowledge that has been accumulated. Then begins the process of filtering what is important to the matter at hand.

Once knowledge has been sifted, the pertinent information can be gathered together, with wisdom being the gift that can then be further filtered to produce clarity. Clarity is not perfect, but it can open the possibility for insights to be gained.

As humans, we think we are pretty smart. We think we know a great many things, but in truth, we know very little. We look at the world around us and we think we know it, but how could we? We look at things and think that they are simple when in truth, they are enormously complex. If we make the mistake of thinking that things are simple, then we risk thinking that they don't matter, and we couldn't be more wrong.

Take a tree for instance. Go ahead. Take a moment to look at a tree. You may look at a tree outside your window and tell yourself that you know that tree. But you are lying to yourself if you think that you do. And at this moment you may actually be defending yourself. "What the hell is she talking about?" you might be thinking. "Of course I know that tree, I have been looking at that tree for years."

But do you really? Of course you know that it is a tree, or at least that is what humans have decided to call it, but simply giving something a name does not mean that you know it. In fact, it may be doubtful that you even know what kind of tree it is. Is it really a tree at all? Do you have any idea how old it is, or how many windy days and nights it has lived through? Do you know how many leaves grow on its branches; is it the same number every year? Do you know how many birds have rested on its boughs?

Do you know if a human planted that tree or if a bird planted that tree or if the wind brought the seed of that tree from a distant land and dropped it in that place so that the tree that you think you know could be there before you now? You don't know at all, but the tree does. Mother Earth knows each and every one of the trees that nestle their roots within Her Flesh.

Every day we delude ourselves into thinking we know what we don't know. And why, you might ask? More than likely, you have never taken the time to ask. Introduce yourself to the world around you. When you finally recognize that as humans we really know very little, you just might begin to learn something. Open your mind and your heart so that you can see what is happening around you.

This beautiful Life is incredibly complex. The smallest ant is enormously complex. The vastness of the sky is enormously complex. And the intricacies of human emotions are enormously complex. So, do yourself a favor when you fiercely defend your position or your motives or your thinking. Pause... Be quiet... Ask... Feel... Learn.

Learn to be a student of Life. And if you are fortunate enough to really have gained some knowledge and wisdom, then humbly offer that knowledge to others, not as a certainty, but as a possibility. It is then up to the individual to allow that wisdom to tumble in their own mind to become a polished jewel that might offer them some clarity. This can neither be forced nor expected - merely hoped for.

Sit for a moment, because if you don't, before you know it you may not have any moments left. If you want to know about Life, be silent, and listen. Life will tell you what you need to know and you will learn that Life is incredibly wonderful.

THE SOURCE OF ILLNESS

*"Never go to a doctor
whose office plants have died."*

Erma Bombeck

Spirit Message
November 21, 2010
2:15 pm

*"Look within you and begin to see that you have held judgment
against others at every turn. You have judged yourself and you
have judged others. Without thinking, judgments are made. She
is this, or he is that. That is good, or that is bad. Judgments have
poisoned your thoughts, your mind and your heart. A poisoned
mind cannot heal. A judging mind cannot find peace. An angry
soul will never find solace. And all of these things bring about
illness.*

*Illness does not come from outside of you rather it comes from
within you. Look this day with critical eyes at the thoughts that
you hold as truth. Know that we say the word critical not cynical
- for there is a great difference in the meaning of these words.*

*It is gall that causes the gall bladder to no longer function prop-
erly. It is a person that will not take in sweetness that begins to*

develop diabetes. It is a person who lives with constant anger and fear that are likely to develop arthritis. Since the liver is a living filter, whose purpose is to filter out what is not needed for health to be maintained, those who do not let things go can easily develop liver failure.

Truly, in order to heal the body, you must heal the mind. And in order to heal the mind, you must begin to heal the heart. To heal the body you must honor the body. To heal a relationship, you must first look at the reality of it and your contribution to its demise or its health.

Know too, that illness is not a punishment, but rather a natural consequence of actions taken.

Know too, that all people will die. There is no escaping this fact. Without death, there would be no end. The end however is a new beginning.

One may experience cancer in a lifetime and die of something else. Rather than fear a disease, care for your Life. For your Life is the Gift. Your Life is your actions and your thoughts and your words and your presence. Your Life is your Gift to Creation.

Sick people die and healthy people die. Good people die and bad people die. Old people die and young people die. The question that you would be wise to consider is... How will I Live?"

The day before my fifty-third birthday I was told that I might have a brain tumor. I had been having some difficulty with pain and tingling and it was getting worse. The day after having an MRI, I received a phone call that made my heart momentarily stop beating. "It looks as though you may have a benign meningioma," I heard the voice say over the phone. "What does that mean?" I fearfully asked. "It means that you might have a brain tumor." I sat in stunned silence. "What should I do?" I asked. "Nothing at the moment, we will just watch it," the doctor replied. How the hell are we going to do that, I wondered.

Walking into the kitchen I shared this news with my husband, as tears slowly fell from my eyes. Suddenly a wall of certainty stood directly in front of me. "Holy shit, I could die from this," I thought. At that moment I knew in no uncertain terms that my Life had an expiration date.

As the days and nights moved by I felt a strange calm come over me. I asked my family to come over so that I could tell them all at one time, so as to be certain to eliminate any speculation and to ask for their continued loving support. My initial reaction was that I was not ready to die and the truth is that I was afraid and I felt that I had so much more work to do. This was not a good time as far as I was concerned.

Curiously, upon visiting physician after physician, it seemed as though my films morphed, as person after person said that they could not see any evidence of a tumor. The pain and tingling persisted but I felt confident that I could live with that. At least I would be living.

Through this time of turmoil I began to realize that I had been given a gift, a gift that, at first glance was unwanted, but ultimately I recognized its value. I realized that my life was my own, and it was up to me to make of it what I will. It brought a deeper confidence in the meaning of what I do and the interactions that I partake in. It gave me the clear and certain understanding that I did not want to waste time on idle nonsense, and it was an impetus for me to let my fears fall away so that I could embrace my journey in this Lifetime.

It also helped me to look very closely at the ways I thought, spoke and interacted with others and with Life. It made me very conscious of the frailty of Life and the fleeting time we have together on this beautiful planet. It opened my senses further and I became more aware of the wounds that others carry and the senselessness of unkindness and fear.

I am happy to say that I do not have a brain tumor, but that one bit of information opened my mind and heart in unexpected ways. Thankfully I have found physicians who are open to different ways of expressing their humanity and can look beyond medical reports to see a human being behind the numbers.

When opportunities for healing present themselves, whether in the diagnosis of a potential brain tumor or in a common cold, please, take the time to recognize the incredible gift this Life is, and in so doing, Live more fully.

THE GIFT OF CHALLENGES

"Pain is inevitable.
Suffering is optional."

M. Kathleen Casey

Spirit Message
November 26, 2010
9:44 am

"It is time to give thanks, truly, time to give thanks. However, we ask that you be thankful for all things. It is the custom for humanity to be thankful for the good things that they have experienced in their lives. Yet we ask that you also, and perhaps more importantly, be thankful for the things that have challenged your mind, your body and your heart. It is that thankfulness that opens you to great and powerful changes.

Life is always giving humanity the opportunity to expand and grow. This growth often comes through the guise of difficulty. For it is through the difficulties of life that you recognize who you are.

Far too often, humanity looks upon events that challenge them as hardships, and can easily become consumed with frustration, anger, resentment and fear. It is in these times of challenge that you can begin to see that it is not so much what is happening to you, or what you are witnessing, but rather, who do you choose to be in relation to all of it. Life is your Teacher, Life is your Counselor and Life is your greatest Gift.

All of you have misunderstood your life challenges. Now it is time to see them for the gifts that they have been. It is time for Thanksgiving for Life has offered you the opportunity to grow. In the midst of hardship you can begin to see whom you choose to be in relation to everyone and everything. Do you choose bitterness, or do you choose peace. Do you choose to be self-righteous or do you choose understanding. You can choose to make a self-determined decision to leave an unhealthy situation so that Life can bring greater love to your experience called Life.

Be thankful this day, and truly every day that you walk upon this Beautiful Mother Earth, in each and every way possible. Thank the sky for its beauty, thank the rain for its life, and thank the warmth of the sun and the brightness of the moon.

Thank the challenges that you have faced so that you can see with new vision. Thank the hurts that you have forgiven, for it opens your hearts to greater love. Thank the losses you have endured, so that you appreciate the richness of the lives you have shared with others. Thank the births that you have witnessed, as you bless those precious brave souls who journey to this Life to experience and express Love in its fullest measure.

Be thankful for your Life, and give it back to Creation at the end of your days as the Gift that your Life has been."

The crowded gymnasium of my son Brian's middle school was bustling with activity. I was there to watch Brian play floor hockey and I loved every minute of his games. In truth it didn't matter to me whether I was watching a practice or a game. I enjoyed watching him play, no matter the sport.

Gingerly climbing up the shaky wooden bleachers I found a vacant spot between book bags, jackets and leggy adolescents. The game was about to begin and I cheered for Brian as he ran onto the court. Throughout the game I heard Brian yell, "Come on, Frankie, you can do it!" Although Brian was a gifted athlete, he made sure that a young man named Frankie got to handle the ball as much as possible. Frankie beamed every time he heard Brian call his name. I cheered them on.

I noticed a woman walking towards me but didn't think much of it. As she approached she asked, "Are you Brian Grohman's mom?" "Yes, I am," I replied. Then she asked, "Can I speak to you, privately? If you don't mind, let's go out into the hall." "Sure," I said as we walked out of the gym and toward the school lockers where we would be able to converse over the roar inside.

As the woman stopped and turned to face me I noticed tears welling up in her eyes. "Are you all right?" I asked. She smiled and said that she was fine. I was puzzled.

"I want to tell you what your son did. And I want to thank you." She began to tell me a story that made tears come to my eyes.

"You don't know me, but I am grateful to you and your son Brian. I have a son named Frankie, and Frankie has special needs. He is mainstreamed into the regular classes and he has always been the subject of teasing, especially in physical education class where he is not as coordinated as the other kids.

Your son Brian apparently noticed that Frankie was being picked on in the gym one day, and Brian made sure that Frankie was included in the game. As time went on Brian continued to be Frankie's protector. He would make sure that Frankie had a chance to throw the ball during games and would cheer him on whenever Frankie had the chance to play. Frankie has never had that kind of support from another student. As you might imagine, he talks about his "buddy Brian" all the time. I wanted to make sure that I talked to you and to thank both you and Brian for his kindness."

I could not take any credit for Brian's actions – he is just that kind of guy. I told her that Brian had a very special aunt, Jackie Pat, my husband's sister, who was profoundly handicapped. He was always protective of her and we always tried to teach him that we all have a responsibility to help those who need assistance, no matter what.
She hugged me and walked back into the gym.

The gym teacher must have heard our conversation and he said, "Mrs. Grohman, I did not mean to eavesdrop on your conversation but I would like to tell you something that has happened here because of Brian. Everyone likes Brian - students, teachers and staff. He has acted as a catalyst, setting an example for the other boys about how they should be treating others. You should be proud."

Still playing on the court Brian turned to me and smiled. My heart nearly burst with pride. When the game was over Brian asked me who the lady was that was talking to me. I told him that she was Frankie's mom and how much she appreciated what

Brian had been doing for her son. Driving home our conversation was light and full of love. I told him that I was so very proud of the way he stood up for someone else. "That's okay Mom, that is what you have taught me to do," he replied.

I later learned that some other boys dared to tease Frankie one day near the lockers. Brian witnessed the event and unflinching walked up to the bully of the group, grabbed him by the collar and lifted him off of his feet, pressing his back against the locker. Brian firmly informed him, "If you ever bother my friend Frankie again, you will have to deal with me. Understood?" It was understood. From that day on, everyone watched out for Frankie and he was treated like one of the guys.

Many years later Brian ran into Frankie. He was happy, healthy and doing well.

As a parent I cannot take credit for my children's actions, but I am always grateful to know that their hearts are open to the needs of others. Just by being himself, Brian has always been an extraordinarily loving little boy, a loving young man, and now a loving grown man. What more could a mother ask for?

life needs
us to
pay attention
to the
reality
of what
is truly important
for
if we fail to
notice anything
what have
we lived for?

Elaine M. Grohman

IN ALL WAYS

"We are all capable of good and evil.
We are not born bad;
everybody has something
good inside.
Some hide it, some neglect, but it is there."

Mother Teresa

Spirit Message
December 9, 2010
1:37 pm

"It is part of the human experience that you will encounter diffi-
cult times, difficult people and difficult circumstances. It is not
wise to ignore them, or pretend to take the high road and simply
live through the difficulty.

Although it can be very painful to witness, it is indeed important
to observe and respond in the most appropriate way. Far too
often, difficult people or circumstances are tolerated, and unwit-
tingly given permission to continue to behave in the manner that
they choose. This, all too often, will begin the cycle of abuse.

Abuse can be overt or subversive, yet its consequence is still the
same...damage to another human heart.

It is time in this point in human evolution that this should no longer be tolerated. Abuse comes in many disguises, and it is not always obvious to the casual observer. Abuse of power attempts to strip another of their value, their sense of worth and their humanity. This should never be allowed.

The most obvious is when there is physical abuse. We can see the wounds of a battered individual, but it is more difficult to see a battered soul. Wounding can come in the workplace, in the home or any place in society.

It takes courage and love to say NO MORE. It takes power to stand up for oneself and say THIS IS NOT LOVE.

Notice each and every day, if you are an abuser. Do you use words to hurt or heal? Do you use resources to allow all to be cared for, or simply a select few? Do you stop another in their words if they are being used as weapons against you? Have you ever used words to control another? We dare say, yes you have!

It is our desire to help you stop this madness, and bring true and lasting healing to your hearts and to your lives. Give praise to those who leave difficult situations where equality is not allowed. Praise the man who walks from a job that causes him to neglect his family. Praise the woman who leaves a man who gives her no regard. Honor the young person who stops a bully on the playground.

You are the only ones who can bring Peace to your world. We, your loving friends, will always guide you, nudge you, support you and stand by your side. But YOU must do it. YOU must make the needed changes. YOU must bring Love forth... forever and in all Ways."

There is a certain look that is observable in an abused person. The eyes avert direct contact, or a minute flinching muscle betrays tension as they brace for a verbal onslaught or swift attack. Their reactions become habitual, and gone unchecked the repetitive responses cause the individual to react to the slightest provocation, both real and imagined. When observing the response to prolonged abuse it is best to remain neutral, asking for neither reason nor confirmation.

A wise man once said to me, "Never reward a problem." At first I did not understand his meaning, yet over time, his wisdom unfolded before me. As I thought of the meaning of the phrase, it became clear that we often have the answers to our problems, laid out before us awaiting our action. The denial of our gift of choice prolongs unnecessary suffering and perpetuates the cycles of abuse. Abuse can be self inflicted or come from an outside source. Abuse that is allowed to continue will destroy everyone and everything in its path.

Within our thinking lie both the problem and the solution. It takes honest evaluation and clear observation of the circumstances for us to make a choice for our own happiness.

For the past few years, I have been invited to be a presenter at a local middle school. The day's events were geared to help students begin to understand some of the pressures and influences that they might encounter in high school. My talk was about Energy Medicine.

During each of the five, fifty-minute sessions I would explain to the kids what Energy Medicine is and give them opportunities to experience energy for themselves. Each group had students who were clearly able to see the energy around one another, and they were fascinated to learn more about it. Interestingly it seemed that each group had one or two kids who seemed to stand out, as if they were willing to be living examples of the information I was sharing with them.

One young woman caught my eye as she slipped quietly into the classroom. Dressed from head to toe in black, she had deep blue-black hair falling onto her face allowing only one eye to be seen. She had tattoos and piercings and looked every bit the tough girl. But looking in her eyes one could see vulnerability - deep wounds that her dark clothes could not conceal.

As I spoke to the group about the Human Energy Field and the work that I do as an Energy Healer her slumped posture began to straighten, cautiously allowing her curiosity to be known. When I asked for a volunteer who might want to have an Energy Healing she quickly raised her hand. Surprised, the others students stared in quiet amazement as she walked to the front of the room. Looking at her closely I noticed marks on her forearms that were telltale signs of self-mutilation. I asked her for permission to touch her and as I did she immediately stated that she felt a strong tingling sensation throughout her entire body. I bent down to whisper in her ear, "How long have you been cutting yourself?" She looked sadly into my eyes and said, "Awhile."

As I continued to demonstrate healing techniques I could see and feel her sadness begin to lift, and the other kids started to enthusiastically relay what they were seeing. As the minutes ticked by this young woman seemed to begin to blossom. Her posture straightened, she brushed the hair from her face and her eyes sparkled with life. She smiled warmly and began to share what she was experiencing with her classmates. "Most people don't know that I have a lot of pain. I can feel the pain leave my body and my muscles don't seem tense. I am not sure what is happening but it feels really good." I smiled and thanked her for sharing.

Before long the session came to an end. As the students shuffled out of the classroom and others were coming in, this young woman came over to speak to me. "Thank you so much," she said, "I can't remember the last time I did not feel this pain. My pain is both physical and emotional, and at the moment, I feel better than I have in my whole life." I was so grateful for this brief encounter and I silently hoped that she would want to investigate life with a more enthusiastic heart.

The final session was over and I walked through the crowded halls preparing to leave. As I turned the corner this same young woman came running up to me, holding the hand of one of her girlfriends. Unceremoniously she wrapped her arms around my neck and gave me a huge hug. "This is the woman I was telling you about," she told her friend. She looked at me and said, "Thank you so much for what you did for me. I now know that I don't have to hurt myself to feel something or as a way to dull my emotional pain. I know that I have to say no to people that are willing to hurt me, and I have to say no to myself when I want to cause myself harm. Thank you so much, I have never felt peace like this in my whole life." I returned her hug and thanked her for being willing to look at Life differently.

Driving home that day, I thanked Spirit for the wonderful opportunity to interact with this beautiful young woman. We never know the wounds that others carry, and since we don't we would be wise to send love to situations and people that we don't understand so that healing can begin to take place. We all cloak ourselves at various times in our lives and it is liberating to set ourselves free to live more fully.

KNOW THYSELF

"The true idea is not opposed
to the real,
but lies in it;
and blessed are the eyes that find it."

James Russell Lowell

Spirit Message
December 27, 2010
9:12 am

"It is the time, dear friends, for you to reflect upon the gifts that
Life has brought to you. Gifts have come to you in many ways,
some that you may not recognize as gifts at all. Those small gifts,
moments that have brought you clarity, are the gift of self-aware-
ness. Self-awareness brings you the greatest gift that you can pos-
sess.

No illusions will bring you peace. No illusions will bring you
joy. No illusions will bring you happiness: all of these things...
peace, joy and happiness can only come from self-awareness.

A moment is all that is needed for you to recognize that you have
spent too much time in self-doubt, self-criticism and self-igno-
rance. When you have moments of self-doubt, rather than dwell
there, ask Your Self plainly, "How can I improve this?" Do not

allow yourself to fall into the illusion that self-doubt will bring you joy. Step out of doubt, for know this Truth, your joy is assured. What is needed for this self-doubt to end and for your Life to truly begin is to make another decision about yourself, and step forward with confidence. It is the joy of wonder and the spirit of creation that helps you to recognize that all is well. Yet nothing will change until you do.

The futile thought of self-criticism has brought nothing to the human heart but misery. Misery is a choice, dear friends, know this Truth. If you have a moment of self-criticism, change it to self-analysis. An analysis thoughtfully surveys the given situation and looks for alternative means of action. Act differently and allow the self-criticism to become self-discovery. That is where the adventure of Living lies.

Never again let self-ignorance be a reason in your life. To Know Thyself is the greatest of achievements. And it is one that is done again and again, moment by moment throughout Life. Knowing Thyself is the greatest gift, for when you know your Self, you know this simple Truth... When you Know Better you will Do Better.

Human Beings are in the midst of a great and wonderful evolutionary change, one of a magnitude not seen in living memory. It is this evolution that is causing humanity to make significant changes in everything about their lives. You too are a part of this change. Let joy and wonder fill your hearts at this time, as the blessing of awareness fills your hearts with a peace beyond your current knowing. Let Love be your Guiding force and all that you see and all that you know will be forever changed by the Love that you bring forth.

Let these moments be gifts to you, precious ones, and let each and every moment hence bring sureness to your thoughts, to your words, to your actions and to your lives. You are here to change this world, and the world that must change first is the world within the chambers of your own Precious Heart. Live Life Fully and know the value in each and every moment and each and every opportunity for self-awareness. You are Important beyond your understanding. Let True Living Begin."

I would like to tell you about an incredible human being. Her name was Elaine Prevost Hughes, and she was my mother. I know, without one single doubt, that she was an Angel here on Earth. She would have blushed to be called that, but it is true. She helped more people in her forty-seven short years than many people help in a lifetime. She did it unceremoniously, with laughter, gentleness and a twinkle in her beautiful, golden amber eyes.

She was born on a cold winter day, Tuesday, December 27, 1921, the first child of Anna and Victor Prevost. Her three siblings, Joe, Gloria and Jimmy would follow her. Material possessions were scarce but growing up during the Great Depression never dampened her spirit. Her treasured father, Victor, somehow made even a childhood illness, which caused her home to be quarantined, into a lovely game. His joy of life became her guidepost, and would serve her well in the years to come.

She led a fairly quiet life, growing up in the city of Detroit and attending St. Cecilia's Catholic School. She loved her family and friends, and if you were lucky enough to have her as a friend, you were indeed lucky enough.

144

One day she met the brother of her best friend Mary Jane. His name was Jack. Jack was a young seminarian who was serious, intellectual and utterly smitten. Before long he made the decision that would change the course of his life. He took off his collar, leaving the seminary behind in order to marry the beautiful, vivacious redhead.

They married in July 1942 and nine months later welcomed the first of their nine children into the world. In short order, the small flat on American Avenue was bursting at the seams, and in 1957, with seven children in tow, they moved to the countryside of Farmington, Michigan. I was their seventh child.

It was a wonderful place to grow up, with acres and acres of nature to explore. It was not unusual to see our neighbor on her beautiful, black horse as they road along the gravel roads of our subdivision. The surrounding hills echoed with the laughter of children. Everyone in the subdivision had large families, and it was easy to count on plenty of playmates.

Within the year Jack and Elaine were delivered devastating news. Their fifth child, Brian Victor, was diagnosed with Duchene Muscular Dystrophy. He was five years old when they were told that it was doubtful that he would reach his twentieth birthday.

Elaine noticed that her husband, Jack was becoming more and more consumed with his demanding career at Ford Motor Company. Elaine was left to tend to the children alone. She baked, played and worked with us, teaching us all to work together as a family. Knowing that her precious boy would die far too soon, she was determined to make the most of every day.

She encouraged each of us to do our best and to learn to be contributing members of the family. Her sense of diplomacy and guidance was evidenced in the way she ran the household, gently guiding our individual abilities and encouraging our strengths.

Each month she would call a family meeting. She was, without question, the CEO. Each of us had to come to the meeting prepared. If there had been a grievance with one of our siblings, we could not just come to the table to complain. We had to write out the problem and then come up with a reasonable solution to the problem. There was always order at the table, and if one of us happened to get upset, she would quietly ask us to remove ourselves from the table until we had regained our composure. She never raised her voice. She didn't have to.

Once all the discussion was complete, she would hand out the monthly job assignments. None of us were exempt from any job, unless of course we were simply too little to do it. Emptying trash, folding laundry, ironing Dad's handkerchiefs, doing dishes or cutting the lawn, it was equal opportunity education, boys and girls alike. No complaining and no argument. Mom was our fearless leader. She would adjourn the meeting, tell us how much she loved us all, and then we would have a popcorn party. She was brilliant!

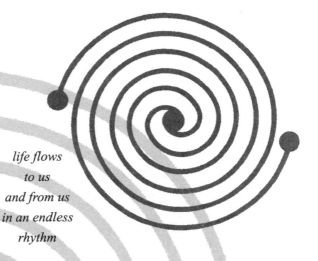

*life flows
to us
and from us
in an endless
rhythm*

*like waves
it flows
allowing us
to expand
and recede*

*keeping
our individuality
yet being
part of
the whole*

Elaine M. Grohman

THE GREAT BEING CALLED
MOTHER EARTH

"This we know;
the earth does not belong to man;
man belongs to the earth.
This we know.
All things are connected like the blood
which unites one family.
All things are connected. "

Chief Seattle

Spirit Message
January 5, 2011
1:41 pm

"Dear Ones, it is time for you to recognize the support that is
waiting for your awareness of its importance to you. The support
that we speak of is so powerful, so benevolent and so amazing
that you will be staggered by the clarity of this understanding.
You stand upon the ground that can heal you, that can change
your pain to peace and that can heal the emotional wounds that
you embrace, and change forever your awareness of the greatness
to which you are intimately connected.

This great and powerful presence has always been known to humanity without being known by humanity. Many before you were clearly aware of the presence of this Great Being, but time and unnatural authority has stripped you of this palpable connection. It is time for that to change, so that truly, you may change.

This great and powerful being has guided your steps, shared breath with you and has given you every conceivable need that you could ever want... yet you do not know this Great Being.

This Being of which we speak is your Mother, your Father, your Grandmother, your Grandfather, your Child and your Friend. It has known all of your ancestors and will cherish all who are yet to be born. This Great Being gives without asking anything in return and does so with more compassion and love than you can fathom.

This Great Being is your Mother Earth. She gives each and every day of your life to you. The air that you breathe is Her Breath. The Land upon which you walk is Her Skin. The beauty that she shares with you as you gaze upon a sunrise or sunset is her Energy Field, Her Aura- from which you are never apart.

In this time of Healing of Humanity, you should introduce yourself to your Mother. You should thank her with each and every breath. You are also being given an opportunity to get to know her children... the trees, plants and animals that support your very Life.

It is Now, in this Time of Great Healing, that you should begin to give back to your precious Mother all that will nourish Her. She has effortlessly and willingly shared with all of Her inhabitants, never asking for anything in return. She cares not where you live, how you live or what you do with your life. She only gives... food, shelter, heat, air... everything. Yet... you give nothing in return.

It is not necessary that you join a group or make a stand with one alliance or another, but rather to Make Your Own Stand count. By this we mean, give to Her what will nourish her. Give Her your sorrow, for to Her it is the substance that enriches her soil. Give thanks, as your good thoughts, words and deeds, which reverberate through Her ethers and spread the Message of Love as it travels forever outward.

Touch the trees. They are magnificent sentient Beings that, once you are known to them, will connect with all trees upon the Earth to help you, no matter where you are.

Talk to your land, the place where you live, and ask that it be a place of peace and harmony. Bless the air that you breathe, for you share that same breath with all of the peoples of the earth, those who are here and those who have come before you.

Bless this Earth, your Precious Mother Earth, and you will be richly blessed in Body, Mind and Spirit. Let it be your new way of being. It will bring you a peace like you have never known and health like you have never felt. It will bring you appreciation for all that is at your disposal, and you will learn to cherish this blessed being, your own Mother Earth. Care for her now, as she has always cared for you. When you bless your environment, you bless yourselves and all who share this Earth with you."

Mother Nature is full of wonderful surprises. When you least expect it, you will be given gifts that open your heart and mind to the incredible interconnectedness of our Living Earth. Experiences with animals are particularly moving and magical.

Recently, I had the opportunity to travel from the United States to Sardinia – a beautiful island in the Mediterranean Sea, off the west coast of Italy. It is a land rich in history, with neolithic and monolithic structures called "nuraghi,"(3) stone dwellings dating from the Bronze Age. These ancient structures dot the landscape, allowing the imagination to drift back in time to envision what life must have been like for those who built and inhabited these structures. They are like empty time capsules on the landscape of Sardinia.

In this magical place I met a fellow creature, a Great Horned Owl to be precise, and felt the power of her presence unlike anything I had ever felt before. I met the Owl through a young woman who was trained in the art of falconry. She brought this magnificent Great Horned Owl to our gathering as a blessing to us all. In Native American tradition, Owl Medicine, the power innate to this magnificent bird, is associated with both Death and Wisdom.

Death can mean more than our mortal lives coming to an end. Death can also represent a release, a changing point of view that allows one belief to drop away so that another, perhaps more open view, can take its place. By replacing old ideas with new ones we open our lives to greater future possibilities.

Owl Medicine also represents wisdom, clairvoyance and the ability to see beyond what is apparent. An owl can see what others cannot, or will not, and can assist in bringing about much needed change. Athena, the Greek goddess of Wisdom, is depicted with an owl on her shoulder, a guardian and friend who would reveal the unseen to her.

Our group was together for the afternoon session when our falconer brought her beloved owl into the room. This magical Being is named Satore-e, which means Wind of the Stars in the Dari language. In the past, they had been unsuccessful in their attempts to have this magnificent bird fly from one side of the room to the other, but they decided to try with our group. They could not force her to do so, but rather asked her if she would be willing. With a simple word they invited her to fly and the graceful creature took flight, gliding silently across the room, its broad wings larger than one might have imagined.

Her large, strong talons could easily have done damage to the delicate human arm she alighted on, but she gracefully rested her weight without damaging human flesh. A second time, she took to the sky, and this time, she flew directly over me.

The feeling was almost indescribable, a rush of tingling sensations raced through my body from head to toes and back again, creating an other-worldly feeling, a momentary shift in dimensions that words cannot explain. It felt like a time-shift had occurred, if only for an instant.

Later that evening I spoke with one of the bird handlers and asked if it was common for the owl to come so close to someone. "You received a blessing, you know," he said with a smile. It's true, it did feel like a blessing, one in which a winged Earth traveler gave a two-legged an expanded perspective of our interconnected world. Indeed, it was a blessing.

Awaiting our flight back to the United States, our falcon mistress caused quite a stir as curious security personnel gathered around the carrier to get a glimpse of this beautiful bird. Our friend opened the cage in order to mist the owl and calm her down from the loud sounds that frightened her. I brought my left hand into the cage and caressed her breast feathers with gentle strokes. She looked at me with her enormous golden eyes and bowed her head to touch her sharp beak gently on my finger. I felt a kinship with this wonderful creature.

Putting my hand down near her feet, she gently touched my hand yet again, this time with her strong, sharp claws. Ever so gently she shared this moment with me, as she blinked her all knowing eyes. I was blessed yet again by her Owl Medicine.

The following morning I awoke in Michigan with the image of the Satore-e eyes in my dreamy mind. In the dark, early morning hour I walked outside and noticed the stillness of the Nature that surrounded me. I raised my hands in the air to greet the coming day, thanking my stalwart, massive maple in the front yard for guarding my home. Just then, a distant "whoo, whooo," greeted me through the darkness. Smiling through joyful tears I returned the call, echoing my gratitude for my inclusion in this magical kingdom that surrounds me. My heart swelled with gratitude.

3. To learn more about the nuraghi, please see the following website:

http://ac-support.europe.umuc.edu/~jmatthew/naples/nuraghipage.htm

BE LOVING TO YOURSELF

"If you treat an individual...
as if he were what he ought to be
and could be,
he will become
what he ought to be
and could be."

Johann Wolfgang von Goethe

Spirit Message
January 19, 2011
3:51pm

"This evening, we ask that you take this message to heart. You are more than you have dared to believe.

Humanity is changing at a rapid pace, with many false illusions falling around your feet. Let illusions fall away so that you can begin to know who you are. Illusions have clouded the minds and hearts of humanity and many have failed to listen to the longing of their hearts. The Heart, your own Precious Heart, is the doorway to Love, the Power that can change all things in an instant.

The human mind has limited itself in the belief that change takes

time, that you are what you have, where you go, what you do and who you know. And we say to you, if you do not know yourself, you do not know Love. The greatest challenge for humanity is self-awareness and self-responsibility. You, dear women, are called to be self aware and self-responsible so those things that have held you bound to wounds and sorrows can be released and you can walk towards your True Self with clear and constant Love.

Far too often judgments have clouded your thinking, and you believed yourself to be someone other than who you are. Your true nature is Love in every molecule of your being. For your sake ask yourself one question, over and over again. Am I being Love right now? And the one that you must Love first is yourself! Love of self is not selfish, but rather, Love of self honors all. And when you honor yourself with Love you stop the endless cycle of little thinking. Anger held within becomes resentment, which can lead to little thinking. Judgment that stops you from moving forward is little thinking. Honor yourself so that nothing less than love will guide you ever again.

Begin to speak to your own precious Self with clarity and honesty. It is only then that the stories that have held you back from knowing yourself will lose their grip on you. When Love is present and Known by the Self, then all things are able to change and blossom.

Speak Lovingly to yourself, and you will speak lovingly to others. Act Lovingly to yourself and you will act lovingly to others. Think lovingly of yourself, and you will think lovingly of others. Then in each moment you finally recognize who you have always been...a Being of Love."

Jack Hughes was a formidable man. He came from humble be-
ginnings, the first-born child of Irish immigrants born on American soil. As the first and only boy, his life, it seemed, was
predestined for the priesthood. It was tradition in an Irish
Catholic home that at least one of the male children would become a priest. It was this directive, without his consent, that
shaped much of his character. Jack Hughes was my father.

His parents, Jennie Lernihan and Patrick Hughes had grown up
a mere county apart on the Emerald Isle. Those two counties
however, were separated by the Shannon River, which to some
seemed as wide as the Atlantic herself. Jennie and Patrick never
knew one another in Ireland. It would take a voyage across the
Atlantic Ocean to unite them, in the bustling, harsh city of New
York. Jennie came to join her elder sister Annie, who was employed as a house servant in a wealthy home. The promise of
employment alongside her sister spurred her on. Not afraid of
hard work, she was ready to do whatever it would take for her to
survive in this new and strange land.

At the tender age of nineteen, Jennie left the tiny family home in
the village of Kilmihil, County Clare. Kilmihil means *Michael's
Church*, for the Archangel Michael, who she hoped would guide
her on her journey west. She was the tenth of eleven children,
and life in Ireland was hard. Her parents supported their children
by living off the land. As farmers of the blanket bog,(4) they toiled
long, hard hours in the fields behind the thatched roof home. The
once forested land had been clear-cut, making turf the only plentiful source of fuel from Mother Earth herself. It was backbreak-
ing work, as the bog was cut into bricks and then dried for months
in the earthen building behind their home.

Turf was used for both cooking and heating, and its thick, pungent aroma hung heavily in the Irish air. Jennie didn't realize how much she would miss the smell of it.

Feeling she had little choice, Jennie made the difficult decision to leave her family, knowing full well that her survival depended upon her willingness to leave the desperate poverty of Ireland behind. Her brave, young heart was moving toward an uncertain future, and her fierce Irish stoicism would rarely betray her fears.

My grandfather, Patrick Hughes, had come to the United States for the first time as a stone carver, under the employ of an English firm. Patrick had grown up surrounded by sharp carving tools, mallets and heavy slaps of stone. Half of the tiny, thatched roof dwelling in the village of Shanagolden, in County Limerick, was home, the other held massive stone slabs, awaiting the skilled hands that would transform them into magnificent Celtic crosses. The Hughes men were known for their elaborately carved Celtic monuments, memorials and headstones, some of which were the only proof of a man's existence. Intricately carved, these Celtic gravestones stood like sentinels over buried bodies, often the most elaborate possession the family had ever owned.

Patrick was one of the many craftsmen from Ireland who were gathered together and sent to dangle perilously over the streets of New York City, wielding chisels and hammers as they worked for hours above the clamor of the noise and filth below. For two years, Patrick labored, carving elaborate facades on the faces of the buildings of New York City. When the contract was concluded, all the Irish were sent back to their homeland, not staying one moment longer than their contract allowed.

Making the long ocean voyage back to his village of Shanagolden, Patrick knew that he would not stay in Ireland for long. As soon as he could make arrangements, he booked his passage back to the United States, where he lived for the remainder of his life.

Once in the United States the Irish stuck together for both safely and some semblance of home. Through friends, Patrick met Jennie, the hardworking daughter of turf farmers, and soon they were married. They stayed for a time in Buffalo, New York but before long Patrick left Jennie behind as he traveled west to a place called Detroit, where he had heard that jobs were plentiful. He promised to secure a job and a residence before sending for his young bride.

He sent her a letter to let her know that he had bought them a home, near Grand River. Harking back to her memories of the Shannon River, she replied with a stern letter admonishing him, asking how in the world he thought they could afford to buy a boat. He had been misunderstood; he meant to explain that Grand River was an avenue, one of the main thoroughfares in the city of Detroit. Relieved, she traveled to Detroit to begin a new life amidst a community of fellow Irish immigrants. Detroit would remain her home for more than fifty years.

Patrick secured a position as a member of the Detroit Fire Department, at a time when horse-drawn rigs were being replaced by more modern fire trucks. His strong, broad shoulders made him suitable for the job. Working long, hard hours in dangerous situations toughened his already tough personality. They settled in a large home on a street named Monica.

It was on Monica Street, on Wednesday, the ninth of April, nineteen hundred and nineteen, that Jennie gave birth to their first child; John Patrick Hughes. They would call him Jack.

Jack was an exceptionally intelligent child, yet his intellect was also a burden. Two years after his birth, his first of two sisters was born. Mary Jane was a quiet child, who was less burdened than Jack by the expectations of their parents, that is, until the birth of their younger sister, Anna. Anna was born with special needs. In those days, she was referred to as mentally retarded. As Jack and Mary Jane easily flourished in school, Anna was kept at home and never entered school until the age of eleven.

Difficulty arose from the social pressures of having a retarded child. It was common in those days, to send a child away to live in a mental institution, far from the glare of judgment and shame. But Jennie and Patrick refused, and the difficult task of educating Anna fell to her older siblings, Jack and Mary Jane.

Growing up I was aware that my father had an unspoken resentment towards Anna that was hard to understand. I observed his demeanor with her as being either short tempered or indifferent, but never warm and affectionate. She was sweet, but there were times when she could be very difficult. It was in my Aunt Mary Jane's later years that she told me the cause of their grief. In their youth, it fell upon the shoulders of Anna's older siblings to try to teach her what they had learned in school. The task was impossible, and if Anna did not comprehend the lessons, Mary Jane and Jack, in particular, were punished for being poor teachers. My father never spoke of this. He would only say, "You have no idea, daughter, how difficult my mother's life was." He was loyal to his mother, even through her impossible demands.

My father's intellect propelled him at a rapid pace through the educational system. His sister, Mary Jane, once boasted that my father had only received one B in his entire educational career. As she relayed the story, all that I could do was close my eyes in disbelief. My aunt told me that on the day Jack received the B, she cried all the way home from school, fearful of the punishment that he would receive. She never shared whether he was punished or not, and truthfully, I did not want to know.

My father never spoke of these things, and in fact, he rarely spoke of his life at all. It was difficult to engage him in conversation, other than superficial or business like matters, but I persevered. One particularly difficult day, I told my father that I wanted him to know me before I died, since at times his indifference was killing me. My persistence finally paid off when eventually, near the end of his life, I was allowed to enter his private world.

(4) To learn more about the Blanket Bogs of Ireland, please see the following website:

http://www.wesleyjohnston.com/users/ireland/geography/bogs.html

THE UNEXPECTED

*"Who has not tasted what it bitter
does not know what is sweet. "*

German Proverb

Spirit Message
January 20, 2011
5:09 pm

*"Life is full of the unexpected. Events and experiences that you
had not anticipated can squarely land in your lap. You attempt
to plan, to cajole and to desire an outcome, yet are often surprised
when the unexpected happens.*

*Truly you should know that everything should be seen as the Un-
expected. Do not let your first response to this statement cause
you to fear, for in truth, no one knows what the next moment may
bring.*

*Rather than worry, let Life unfold before you into the magical ex-
periences that they will be. Let the unexpected bring you joy and
a state of wonder so that you may be more fully alert to the gifts
that your life brings to you.*

Let the Unexpected be what you come to expect, and you will be filled with amazement, curiosity, joy and love. You will then be able to know that Life is comprised of countless unexpected moments that can bring you closer to the understanding of who you truly are. Witness the big and the small, the strong and the weak, the old and the young.... witness it all as the gift of Life unfolding for you. And treasure the Unexpected, for that is where Life's greatest treasures often lie."

Jack always respected the wishes of his parents, even if his heart longed for something more. Because of his high intellect, Jack was advanced two full grades, allowing him to graduate from Sacred Heart Seminary High School at the age of fifteen. He was immediately enrolled in Sacred Heart Seminary where he received both his religious education and his college degree. He once told me that being in college at fifteen was a sense of pride for his parents, but extremely difficult for him. He was a slightly built youth, quiet and studious. He looked like a child amidst the college freshman, and he found it difficult to make friends. He was quiet, serious, determined… and a genius.

Then one day, tragedy struck. His father was working in the back yard of their home on Monica Street, caring for the firehouse's Dalmatians, when he slumped over the doghouse, dead of a massive heart attack at the age of fifty-two. My father's younger sister Anna just happened to be looking out her bedroom window and screamed when she saw her father fall. She was the first to reach his side, and became inconsolable when she realized that he was dead.

It was rare for my father to reminisce about happy times in his family home, so when he did, I would listen intently. He told me that on Friday nights, the living room of the home on Monica Street became something special. It was my father's job to move the furniture and roll up the rug, transforming the living room into an Irish pub, where his parents' friends played fiddles and danced Irish jigs until the wee hours of the morning. It was one way to reconnect with the villages and traditions they had left behind in Ireland.

But on this day Jack came home to dutifully move furniture and roll up the rug for a different event – his father's wake. Patrick knew people from all walks of life, including those whose livelihoods were less than favorable to an Irish Catholic woman. All day and through the night people streamed into the cramped living room in order to pay their respects to Patrick and his grieving family. My father stood by his mother's side, knowing for certain that now he was responsible for the care of his mother and sisters.

Patrick died on his day off, not in the line of duty as a fireman, so my grandmother did not receive his pension. She would have to make a living by taking in boarders and doing laundry. In those days laundry was done by hand, using a heavy corrugated metal washboard and a hand-cranked wringer. It was back breaking work, especially considering the soot and grime that would be on the clothes of the factory workers who became her boarders. The clothes were always cleaned, starched and pressed, including sheets and linens.

Grandma Hughes insisted that her son stay in the seminary, coming home on weekends to visit and to help with household chores. One weekend, his sister Mary Jane needed a ride home from a local dance. Jennie instructed her son to drive to the dance to bring Mary Jane home. Arriving at the school, Mary Jane asked her brother if he would mind giving her friend, Elaine Prevost, a ride home. He agreed. Within moments of meeting the beautiful, bubbly red head with electrifying amber eyes, he knew that he would never become a priest, and he also knew that there would be hell to pay. By this time he already was wearing a collar, but the chokehold of it was about to be withdrawn. He hoped that he would be able to withstand his mother's fury, and was grateful that he did not have to explain this career change to his father.

SELF LOVE, SELF AWARENESS & SELF RESPONSIBILITY

*"When you have to make a choice
and don't make it,
that is in itself a choice."*

William James

Spirit Message
January 28, 2011
4:57 pm

"Dear Friends, illusion has clouded the thinking of humanity almost to the point of madness, and we, your Angelic guides and friends would like to help you look away from your illusions so that you can truly begin to see the wonder and the beauty that Life provides for you.

When we speak of illusions we want you to know that each and every one of you live in illusion. You all have believed yourselves to be weak, to be small, to be right, to be wrong...all of it, and it has brought heartache and disillusionment to your days.

We wish to assist you in seeing your Life anew, as the beautiful and wondrous gift that it is. Your Life is the single most remark-

able gift that you will ever receive; yet few see this truth. Rather, you run from yourself, seeking to fill your time with things that are of little consequence.

The illusions that we ask you to release are those that have prevented you from knowing yourselves as the powerful beings that you are. And the first power that will spark your life is the gift of knowing yourself. As you begin to know yourselves, you will realize that you have not always been truthful. You believe yourself to be victims of time and circumstances and this has held you bound to your wounds.

Begin to see that what makes you angry or afraid is never meant to hold you fast, but rather to cause you to pause and examine what is important to you. And let it be known that the most important thing for any human is Self Love, Self Responsibility and Self Awareness. These things, once truly known will release you from anger, resentment and from old histories that have played over and over in your mind. Let this mindless chatter cease so that you can make a decision for Love's sake.

Love is the great equalizer, the great healer and the greatest self-gift. Love brings you clarity and peace. Love brings you determination and awe. And love brings you the wisdom to follow Love's path once and for all."

My father eventually left the seminary to marry my mother, Elaine Prevost. His mother was so unhappy that she wore a black dress and a black veil to their wedding. My dad later became a purchasing executive for the Ford Division of Ford Motor Company and was highly regarded for his integrity, hard work and intelligence. He was a mathematical genius with a photographic memory and nothing regarding business escaped his notice.

Jack and Elaine had nine children. I am their seventh child. With five girls and four boys the house was always bustling with life and love. Their fifth child, our brother Brian, was diagnosed with Duchene Muscular Dystrophy at the tender age of five. Our father did not take the news and prognosis well and he gradually became distant from his children, fearing the pain of becoming too close, knowing full well that his beautiful son would die. I was twelve years old when Brian died. He was just about to turn sixteen. Fourteen short months later, our precious mother died three days after having surgery. She was forty-seven years old. I was just thirteen, when the love of my life was taken from me.

In 1972, when I was sixteen years old, my father married a woman named Jane Wolford Hughes, the widowed mother of seven children. They had a total of fifteen children between them. I went from being the seventh of nine children to the twelfth of fifteen in our newly blended family. Our families did the best we could to blend our many lives together. It was not an easy transition, but thanks to the foundation of love that our mother had shown us, the fabric of the Hughes family remained strong, in honor of the lessons of Love our mother taught us.

WHAT DO YOU FEEL?

"Faith is the bird
that feels the light
and sings
when the dawn is still dark."

Ravindranath Tagore

Spirit Message
February 20, 2011
9:29 am

"Consider the consequence of not being True to yourself. No longer deny what you feel, how you feel and the impact of the situations you find yourself in.

It is important and indeed imperative that you recognize what is going on outside of you, but most importantly, what is going on Inside of you. Consider what you Feel.

Many of you misunderstand your own feelings. We are not speaking of your habit of emotional reaction, but rather, what do you FEEL?

By using the gifts of your senses, you can navigate your life more fully. Do not use your feelings and emotions to manipulate oth-

ers, but rather use them to truly FEEL.

Your true use of your emotions will open brilliant opportunities for insight, clarity and helpful actions in your own life. By using your Feelings in the most appropriate way, you will learn to navigate the waters of life, rather than creating turbulence in your wake.

Your Feelings are guideposts that should not be ignored, nor should they be confused with your emotions. Learn to discern the difference and your life will open for you in New and Beautiful Ways."

I had just concluded teaching a weekend workshop of Sacred Geometry and Energy Medicine Level I. The workshop was held at a major metropolitan hospital and was attended by nurses as well as others interested in learning about healing. It had been a powerful weekend in which participants experienced Energy Healing in very palpable ways. Many commented that they had never had such a profound experience of feeling and seeing energy before. A few days later, I received the following email from Mary N., one of the nurse participants in the weekend workshop.

"… This happened on the evening of our last day of class for Sacred Geometry and Energy Medicine Level I - Healing From the 4th Dimension. It was Sunday, January 16, 2011.

A good friend named Sue called that evening "just to hear my voice." She was scheduled to have bilateral knee replacement surgery the following morning and admitted that she was very nervous, although she really trusted her doctor. She had suffered for four long years with excruciating knee pain, which greatly impacted her quality of life. As we spoke, I told her about the class I had just taken.

I offered to do a "treatment" over the phone, in which I would guide her through the process as we spoke. After working with energy for over fifteen years, I thought, "Why not? Miracles happen every day!"

So I used my "energy doll" as a surrogate for Sue and began the healing session. While I was working I sensed four Spirit Beings around her plus Archangels Michael and Raphael. We talked for about twenty minutes as I was doing the treatment. When we were finished I said goodbye and I wished her luck, letting her know that I would stop by to see her after surgery the following day.

Five minutes later the phone rang. Sue was yelling into the phone. "I can't believe this – look," she shouted to her family and me. "I am walking with NO PAIN!" Her husband got on the phone and told me that she was not using her cane nor did she have her familiar limp. Sue then went to the stairs to get something from the basement (while I was still on the phone), and she was able to go up the stairs like a "normal" person, not dragging herself up one step at a time and with absolutely NO PAIN. "I haven't been able to do that for four years!" Sue exclaimed. We said our goodbyes once again.

The next day I visited Sue at the hospital and although she was groggy, she was feeling comfortable. She asked me to give her another treatment, which I gladly did. I then asked her how long had she been able to walk without pain after the previous evening's session. She told me that she had walked into the hospital that morning with no pain and... no cane!"

The wonderful thing about healing is that it doesn't always take a long time. In fact, many times a change can occur in a matter of minutes, forever altering the perspective of those involved. When the unexpected occurs, our hearts and minds expand to include that which we had previously thought was impossible. And it is then that we can begin to witness Life with a sense of wonder as it unfolds its secrets before us.

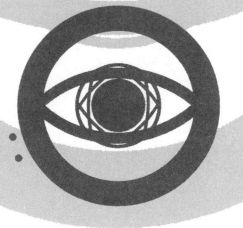

look again
and
then
see

Elaine M. Grohman

SEEDS OF CHANGE

"It is the commonest of mistakes
to consider that the limit
of our power of perception
is also the limit of all there is to perceive. "

C. W. Leadbeater

Spirit Message
February 23, 2011
12:53pm

"Spring is on its way. Although you may not recognize this, your own Spring is also on its way.

As the beauty of the snow allows for peaceful slumber, beneath the snow lie the seeds of possibility. We, your Angelic friends, have watched you as you have planted seeds of possibility that lie dormant, waiting for the perfect time to begin to take root.

The Seeds of Possibility have great potential to spring to Life when the conditions are right for growth. Begin today, in this hour, to recognize what seeds you have sown that will soon be coming to Life.

Keep in Mind that there are seeds that bring forth Life, and seeds that can choke off Life... which have you planted?

Your words, thoughts, actions and deeds are the Seeds of Possibility that you Sow in your own Life. But know this clearly, that the seeds you plant not only affect your Life but also the lives of those around you.

It is time for you to recognize the seeds that you plant, each and every day, and the magnificent potential or the unnecessary harm that may come. The choice is yours. Nurture the Love that Brings Life forth, in your own Hearts and in the Hearts of those around you, not only for your loved ones, but the whole of humanity, from which you are never separated.

Be the Gardener of your Life, nurture riches and love that will bring greater value than any material wealth can ever offer. Sow all of your thoughts with Love and Care, Patience and Trust and with the sure knowledge that You can create and you can destroy... be very mindful of that Truth.

Let your Love be like a blanket of freshly fallen snow, gently protecting and nurturing the seeds of possibilities you have planted by your Love. Nurture yourself and others so that your Life will be a magnificent garden of possibilities."

Human beings seem to have forgotten about the future, and the future that we have neglected to consider is here, right now. Is it any wonder that we have allowed ourselves to be so forgetful?

We spend so much time looking down - looking down at a computer, looking down at a cell phone and looking down at one another. What we need to do is to start looking up. Look up to the sky, look up to the mountain, look up to the trees and start to remember one very important thing. All of it, every star, every ocean, every stream, every blade of grass, and every species of creature have been here long before us.

All of Creation - everything that we are able to see, as well as the millions upon millions of things that we will never see, know, or begin to understand, was here on this Earth long before humanity came along. A tree has never damaged the Earth. A rock has never withdrawn its strength from us. The sky has never selectively displayed its beauty for only a privileged few. The beauty of the sky is here for all of us to love and appreciate.

The beauty of a planted seed may take years to bear fruit, but steadfast attention along with lots of Love will help plants display their bounty in the most precious ways. Our daughter and son-in-law's first-born child is a precious boy named Conner. As an infant, each time I would change his diaper I would direct his attention to the trees and garden outside. We would look out the window together and I would say, "Good morning trees, thank you for your beauty." And as I was preparing him for bed, I would say, "Night, night trees, thank you for your beauty. Night, night stars thank you for your light. Night, night birdies, thank you for your songs. Night, night everybody!" It was my hope that these simple phrases would begin to help him appreciate the wonder of Nature and all that She provides.

One day I received a beautiful message from my daughter, Lainie. "Mom, I had to call to tell you something. This morning, as I was changing Conner, I opened the window shade, and in a clear, precious voice Conner looked out the window and said, "Good morning twees, thank you for your beauty."

Now Conner is telling his baby sister Isabella, "Good morning twees, thank you for your beauty," as he effortlessly passes along the appreciation that we all need to be aware of.

Appreciation for what supports our lives are the blessings that we offer back to Creation for the Gifts that Life continually brings. Now, each morning, Conner also sleepily walks over to the fish tank and says good morning to his fish.

YOU ARE NOT YOUR HISTORY

"Life belongs to the living,
and he who lives
must be prepared for changes."

Johann Wolfgang von Goethe

Spirit Message
February 25, 2011
5:09 pm

"Dear Friends, we, your Angelic Friends and Companions on this journey called Life, would like for you to begin to release yourselves from the limited thinking of your experiences and history. Know clearly in this hour that you are not your history. You are not a reflection of things done or said by others. It is time for you to know that you have the beautiful opportunity to be an expression of yourself, an expression of Love.

For far too long, humanity has allowed itself to be defined by labels of other people's thinking. You must be this...you are just like that... and on and on it goes. You are you, and no other being can be the blessed being that you are.

Each and every glorious moment of your Life you have the opportunity to BE whoever you wish to be. By this we mean you can change your point of view, truly your own view of your life and how you wish to live it. No longer be limited by anger, resentment, worry and frustration. All of those emotions are expressions of limited understanding of Love. Love is the Elixir of Life. Love is the Endless Possibility of Creation and it is yours to Command. Command Love and Love will be expressed by you.

You have believed that your wounds define you, and we say to you truly this is not the Truth. The Truth is that you define you, each and every minute of each and every day of each and every blessed year that you are gifted with. Each and every second is the culmination of your Life. What do you wish your Life to be about?

It matters not where you came from, the only thing that matters is where you are. Where are you in your own Life? Are you a victim or a victor? Are you a creator or a spectator? Your Life is the greatest gift you will ever possess, and in Truth it is your only possession.

Possess Love in your Heart and your Life will be full of Love. Possess charity in your Heart and you will see others through different eyes. Possess the wisdom of non-judgment and you will not feel the sting of others judging you. Possess Integrity and all that you do will be an example of Love for Others.

Create your Day with the Love that is your Birthright. Do it now, and your life will be full and joyful. Far too soon this precious Gift, your Life, will be over. Command Love and Be Love and all that you See and Know will change. That is the definition of a Miracle."

My dad and Jane were married for thirty-two years. He died on December 19, 2003, at the age of eighty-four. We had come along way, my father and I. Near the end of his life, out of necessity and my perseverance, he let down his stoic Irish guard and allowed me to become closer to him. My sister Dianne and I did healing work with him as he was dying, and for one precious moment we witnessed his frail body gain enough strength to raise his arms in the air and gather them to himself in a long awaited embrace. With silent tears he relaxed as one by one all five of his daughters entered the room and stood around his bed as he took his last breath.

Gradually the room filled with all of his children along with Jane and three of her children, his stepchildren. A chapter of my life had ended, but the wisdom of his life and mine had woven together in an unbreakable bond. I finally knew my father and he knew me.

In July of 2004, twelve of us brought a portion of our father's ashes to his mother's ancestral home. All five of Jack Hughes' daughters, four of our husbands, one son and three grandsons stood together on the peat farm in the village of Kilmihil, County Clare, Ireland, to introduce our father to his parents' homeland. The following is an essay that my nephew Matthew had written about his experience.

"This past summer I took a trip to discover my roots, to let my grandpa go and build even stronger bonds with my family. I went to Ireland. The trip consisted of my dad, my brother, five of my dad's sisters and four of their husbands and finally, my cousin Nick. There were twelve of us in all.

We were here for many reasons, but in my eyes, the most impor-

tant reason was to spread my grandpa's ashes on his own family's land. To bring him home. While we were there we also met some relatives that live in Ireland, which was pretty cool.

The first thing that struck me about Ireland was its beauty. Although I have not been to very many places, Ireland is one of the most beautiful places that I have ever seen, both inside and out. The land and the people are gorgeous.

We landed at Shannon Airport in County Clare, which is near the middle of the country, and everywhere I turned I saw rolling hills of every shade of green imaginable. I was amazed to see cows everywhere!

As we headed toward the sea, the scenery changed. There were extraordinary cliffs and breath-taking views. But now instead of cows, there were sheep everywhere. We could see all the white dots standing on the sides of these mountains.

But the thing that struck me the most was the Irish people. We did not encounter a single mean or nasty person there. Everyone was kind and made us feel right at home. Most of the people lived in poverty, or at least the ones I met, but they always offered us something to eat or drink. They always gave what they could and refused to accept anything in return. It was quite remarkable. Americans could learn a little something from the Irish.

Our search for family members was pretty easy. My dad, with his brother and a handful of sisters, had been to Ireland before and had found them. My Aunt Dianne had kept in touch so we knew right where to go. We first met the Lernihan's, my great grandma's family. There we met a very old woman named Christina.

Although I had never met her before, I knew immediately that she was family. I looked into her eyes and saw my grandpa's eyes staring back at me. Upon closer inspection, her facial features closely resembled my grandfather's. It was the strangest thing. This event put everything in perspective for me. Yes, I am really here, and yes, these people are really part of my family.

Later, at the house where my great-grandma was born, we spread out my grandpa's ashes. It was an ironic moment. My grandpa never really expressed any outward desire to go Ireland. He would never say why and I guess he took that secret with him to the grave. In fact for one of his birthdays, my dad and his siblings bought grandpa two tickets to Ireland. He never used them.

The family decided to have one third of his ashes be buried with his first wife, one third be with his second wife, and the final third were to be spread across his parents' homeland.

Letting Grandpa's ashes fly with the wind was very hard for my aunts and father to do. They cried a lot, said a prayer, and finally let him go. My Aunt Maureen took a great close up picture of four hands, belonging to two of my aunts, my father, and my brother, each with some of grandpa's ashes in their hand. As the wind swept them away, I think everyone felt a sense of closure and knew that everything was going to be all right.

After spreading the ashes we continued our journey. We took the ferry to cross the Shannon River, and found our way to the tiny village of Shanagolden. There we met Joan, the last remaining Hughes living in the village. She still owns the house that my great grandpa was born in. It is across the road, as they say in Ireland, from her house. This house was 400 years old and still standing, but it was not in very good shape. Joan had met my dad four years before and her jaw dropped when she answered the door. She could not believe her eyes as she excitedly ushered us in.

We all gathered around a small table as she brought out a crumbling scrapbook that held photographs and writings of my great-great uncle. It turns out he was a tombstone maker. Some of his work was still on Knockpatrick. I also saw a letter describing my great grandfather's death. (He was a fireman in Detroit, and one day he came home, sat down in his backyard, and died of a heart attack. His helmet still hangs in my dad's house.) This was another of those strange occurrences. I have always known how he died, but to see it described on a piece of paper in this woman's house half way around the world was truly bizarre.

After catching up a bit, Joan took us up on Knockpatrick. "Knock" is the Gaelic word for big hill, which was fitting. Knockpatrick is a gigantic hill that oversees both County Clare and County Limerick. Legend has it that this was the spot where Saint Patrick blessed both those counties. More importantly, it is the graveyard where the Hughes are buried. Standing there, looking at my ancestors' graves, knowing for sure that they are in fact my ancestors, not just some coincidence, is really something that everyone should experience, to travel half way around the world, and still be right at home. That is a wonderful feeling and something that I will never forget. I can't wait to go back."

A young man walked on his ancestors' homeland and in that moment was able to begin to view his own life through different eyes. Learning of the past can help us understand our present so that we might walk confidently into a future of our own making.

A WORLD OF YOUR CREATION

"Of one thing I am certain,
the body is not the measure of healing -
peace is the measure."

George Melton

Spirit Message
March 2, 2011
3:57 pm

"Dear Ones, with singular intent we are here to help you begin to love yourselves and therefore love your Life with great and truthful passion. To love your Life means that you respect all that supports your Life. From the beauty of nature to the clean fresh air, all of it must be appreciated so that you can understand the value that it holds for you.

It is imperative that you begin to recognize your responsibility in everything that you do. Far too often, complaints and problems arise and are often blamed upon others rather than looking within yourselves to see your part in things.

No problem arises of its own accord. In order for a situation to be mended and healed, all must look at their contribution to the dilemma. Without honest recognition and ownership of one's contribution, no lasting and fruitful solutions can be attained.

We ask you to look at all of the situations in which you find your-self immersed in conflict, whether that conflict is in your own homes, in your workplace, in your community or in the whole of humanity. You have had a part to play in it all, even if you do not recognize that fact. Stop for one moment and do not point your finger at another, but rather stand in quiet contemplation and look at your own actions or inactions that may have contributed to the discord. It is only through honesty that peace can be at-tained.

Even within your own human heart, we observe the conflict of untruth. Be truthful with yourselves about everything - your feel-ings, your reactions, your needs and your dreams. Step confi-dently into that moment of creation with an honest and loving heart, for that is where change occurs and that change may be the change you have been praying for. We love you and respect you more than you do yourselves. Look again with loving eyes on the lives that you live. It is only in that place of Peace that you can step into a New World of your own creation."

We all know people who refuse to take responsibility for their ac-tions. They become locked in a never-ending cycle of self-indul-gence, filling their lives with mindless things, wasting time with battle games and buying endless amounts of stuff in the hopes that it will bring some satisfaction. It never does. It never can.

We have believed the hype that we must always have the latest and greatest, and if possessing one of something is good, then having one hundred must be better. We have created hoarding mentalities that have buried us in an avalanche of things. Because of this thinking we are stuck with tons and tons of plastic articles that eventually end up in landfills, and then we buy more to replace what we have just disposed of.

Simplicity is not simple, but simplicity allows us room to breathe. With fewer things to distract us from living, we can create opportunities to appreciate our lives more fully. Relearning how to appreciate individual things, one at a time, can serve to open our creative imaginations and unlock untold treasures yet to be discovered. Perhaps we could rethink the concept that more is better. Maybe it's time to let some things go.

When we begin to simplify our lives we begin to interact with one another again. Reducing endless amounts of toys and gadgets can free us from the prison too many things can create. We can then make time for one another so that we can engage in meaningful conversations and teach our children and grandchildren the importance of Life rather than have their childhoods fly by in the mindless interaction with inanimate objects.

Take a child to a farm, so that they can begin to understand that their food really comes from Mother Earth, not from the local super market. Teach children to plant a garden, so that they learn to appreciate patience, care and enjoy the wonderment of watching plants grow and eventually produce something that will sustain life. Walk with a child through the woods so that they can begin to appreciate the magical sounds of Nature and the aromas of the Earth.

We owe it to ourselves to change in order to bring about balance. We are terribly out of balance, and our world is suffering because of it.

Innovation comes from a creative mind, not a mind muddled with useless information and endless games of destruction. Our Earth is crying out for our attention, and we have to lift our head up to see the mess that we have created. Only then can we see the faces of those around us, know that we are in this together and begin to build a healthier world.

all things are
connected
in the web of life
we can never be
separated
from
our world
or ourselves
and if we think
we are
it is only an illusion

Elaine M. Grohman

The Threshold
of the Miraculous

"Unified, disciplined, armed with the secret powers
of the atom and with knowledge
as yet beyond dreaming,
Life, forever dying to be born afresh,
forever young and eager,
will presently stand upon this earth
as upon a footstool and stretch out its realm
amidst the stars."

H. G. Wells

Spirit Message
March 23, 2011
4:35 pm

"Humanity's greatest hour is here, unlike any time in human history. You stand at the brink of the awakening of the human heart and this is beautiful to behold. The moment is now, as humanity cannot sustain itself in a perpetual state of turmoil without the body, mind and spirit being adversely affected.

Each human being comes to a point of ultimate Truth when they recognize, perhaps for the first time, that they will not be in their physical body forever. Illness and death can bring us squarely to the point of balance, and thus offering the opening of the doorway to the Heart in the truest sense.

The Heart is the Threshold of the Miraculous and the place where all pretenses are thrown aside and the beauty and mystery of Life can be experienced and expressed. To stand upon that threshold is the place where True Living begins. It is here that the gift of this Life is appreciated and savored. It is here that all false images are rendered useless. It is here that you recognize your capacity to change.

Yet we wish to assure you that you can stand within that threshold at any time, in any moment without the need for illness or death to bring you there. Between each heartbeat, there is a fraction of time where you are no longer animated. In the space between breaths, you momentarily stop, albeit it almost imperceptibly. Yet you are dying in every moment, and also living in the next. Bring your awareness to your living, to your loving, to your open and forgiving heart so that humanity can put its collective weaponry down and walk together in Peace."

I am a student of Life. My eager mind is willing to explore new territory, opening me to new and wondrous experiences that further propel me into wanting to understand more. Many of us are stopped before we begin when we ask for "proof" of what exists around us. Quieting our own thinking, we might just begin to understand that all that exists for us does not need our understanding to exist, but, if we are truly interested in exploring the secrets that Life holds, Creation will push the doors of understanding wide open, allowing us to step into the wonder of the world that surrounds us.

I was listening to a dear friend speak to a group of people about the importance of understanding our intimate connection to Nature. Her voice was filled with love and appreciation for all that she holds dear. She was asking all of us to consider the same. As a Teacher of the Sacred Truths of Mother Life, her superior, humble intellect, coupled with her masterful articulation of the spoken word, was eclipsed momentarily by the beautiful sight before my eyes. I stood transfixed, as I watched a soft glow of pale green light begin to surround her and illuminate her body.

She sat surrounded by live potted chrysanthemums, beautifully displaying their colors of golden yellow, deep red and brilliant white. A smaller pot contained happy pansies, their yellow, white and violet faces smiling at the group gathered there.

As she spoke of our intimate connection with Nature, she reminded all of us to begin to talk to Mother Earth, and to the beauty that Nature provides. Trees, flower, birds and animals are all connected to one another and to ourselves. This is a fact that we have forgotten, and in that forgetfulness, we have lost our own connections. We have given ourselves permission to neglect our responsibilities for care of this beautiful planet, and without Her we cannot survive.

Her eloquence and heartfelt words resonated deeply within me and was further solidified by the incredible sight that was unfolding before my eyes. The golden chrysanthemum behind her began to pulsate with energy, looking very similar to the heat that emanates from hot asphalt. Suddenly, the heat waves vanished and the area surrounding the chrysanthemum began to pulsate with deep violet and cobalt blue light. The light extended 6-8 inches from the vibrant flowers. As the teacher spoke, her aura began to take on the same violet hues, encapsulating her pale green glow with the added color.

Suddenly, the violet light from the chrysanthemum's glow moved towards the speaker and gently began to encircle her torso with its Light. I was unable to move and could barely breathe, as I stood transfixed and unwilling to make any sudden moves, wanting to savor the sight. I had seen auras many times before, but never had I seen such intensity of color or the interaction of a Living Plant with a Human Being. There are no words to adequately describe the event.

I knew with certainty that this happens all of the time, yet we neglect to notice and therefore we deny what we can see. I have known this feeling before, as I have spent countless hours in my own garden, surrounded by the beauty and comfort that Nature provides. I have shed tears, I have laughed and I have worked the soil around our home for many years, and the fruits of those times have blessed us with its spectacular beauty.

I urge you to begin to appreciate the Life that surrounds you, for without it, our very breath would cease. It is time for us to be multi-lingual beings, adding the voice of Creation to our own, and inviting It to enrich our Lives in extraordinary ways.

BE LIGHT HEARTED

*"Your vision will become clear
only when you can look into your own heart.
Who looks outside, dreams;
who looks inside, awakes."*

Carl Jung

Spirit Message
April 4, 2011
11:44 am

"Look with wonder at the beauty of your life. The heartfelt appreciation of your years of existence will be a gift to you and to others.

With a heart full of wisdom and love, we ask that you share that love and wisdom with others.

Some of you feel that life is not fair, that you have lost those most dear to you. Remember and treasure the gift each life brings so that bitterness and grief no longer cloud your judgment.

For those who struggle with pain, bring comfort. For those who struggle with suffering, bring your heart. Suffering is of the mind where as pain is of the body.

195

Suffer not with wounds of old. Release them to the Light. All suffering clouds wisdom from being present. Let the appreciation of Life be what you choose to focus upon. All of humanity is here but a short time. Use your time with love, compassion, generosity, forgiveness and humor... and your Heart will be Light Hearted and your journey appreciated."

———————————

Sitting in the living room surrounded by women, my heart began to feel a deep heaviness. I had never been to this home before and each face was unfamiliar to me. Yet there was recognition of the palpable energy of oppression. Sitting across from me was a quiet woman, whose eyes were downcast, her expression blank.

After reading the above Spirit Message prepared for them that evening, I began to receive messages for each individual. When my attention was directed to the woman seated across from me, an overwhelming sense of urgency filled my being. "Is someone hurting you?" I asked. She shook her head no. I asked again, "Is someone hurting you?" This time, she began to cry. One of the women in the group urged her to speak the truth. Spirit showed me that she was being abused, both physically and verbally, and that her life had become an endless tangle of angry words and put-downs.

This was the perfect place to have Spirit bring this out in the open, surrounded by women who loved her and wanted her life to be free of the shackles of abuse. By the end of the evening the woman's demeanor had completely changed. Before the end of the night, she came to me and gave me a hug, thanking me for bringing this out in the open. She no longer needed to hide behind the wall of shame, for the truth was this was not her shame, but the shame of her abuser.

Among the women at that evening's gathering, one woman sat quietly holding her young daughter. It was clear that the toddler had some disabilities, but I was uncertain as to the extent of her handicap. The mother approached me, asking if I would be willing to do some energy healing with her baby girl. This sweet little one came into my arms without fuss and I carried her to the adjacent room and laid her on the plush carpet.

Working gently with her she smiled and began to giggle. Within a few minutes, I helped her to sit and she waved her arms excitedly in the air. Her mother stood by as I explained to her what she could do for her child. Sitting together on the floor the mom began to cry, telling me that her little one had never been able to sit up by herself before. I was dumbstruck, since she seemed to have little trouble sitting comfortably on the floor.

I taught the little girl's mom the simple techniques that would help the natural energy of the Earth run through her child's body. The baby smiled and my heart beat a little faster with the sure knowledge that more things are possible than we might believe.

first you must
glean knowledge
then you must gain clarity
then and only then
will you have wisdom
this wisdom will allow
you to see with
different eyes

Elaine M. Grohman

THE WONDER OF IT ALL

*"Sooner or later every one of us
breathes an atom that has been breathed before
by anyone you can think of
who has lived before us -
Michelangelo or George Washington or Moses."*

Jacob Bronowski

Spirit Message
May 2, 2011
12:43 pm

"Let your Light shine. It is time to let your Light shine.

Within each and every cell of your Being there is a spark of Light. If you were able to look even deeper into the molecular structure of your cells you would know and see your Light. This Light is dynamic, instructive, all encompassing and the source of information for your body, mind and spirit. It is the Light of Love and the Light of God. Is the language of the cosmos that permeates through your system, igniting its multitude of actions and interactions in perfect harmony of design.

Stepping back from the minute essence of your own quantum levels of existence you begin to witness the delicate yet intricate Light emissions that make up the totality of your being.

It is known that our Creator/Creatress thought and therefore in-voked the concept – "Let there be Light." And in that Beautiful and Powerful statement of intent, the whole of the Universe was activated into the magical expression of Communication through Light. Light is not simply the opposite of dark, but rather is the delicate interaction, both in minute detail and the vastness of the cosmos that instantaneously transmits information in microseconds of Time.

Let your Light Shine. It is time to actively use the Light within you to create the Life that you wish to Live. Let Light shine from you and guide your every move. That Light is Love. That Light is Goodness, that Light is Creation in action. That Light is you. Let there be Light. Be the Light that you are meant to be, now and forever."

The Universe was created through the principles of Balance. At this moment in Human history we have very little equilibrium, and we are paying the price for that imbalance. Balance requires an honest evaluation, a steadiness that once attained, can allow for a smoother flow of events in life thus facilitating the understanding and comprehension of our need for stability.

There cannot be an up without a down; there cannot be an east without a west. There is no day without the night. Everything needs balance and therefore everything has an integral part within the Whole. Any loss in the fabric of Life could be the thread that begins to unravel the structure that supports us. Unseen does not mean unnoticed.

We are out of balance in the physical world, especially in relationship to our Earth. We have used more natural resources in the last one hundred years than had been used in all previous centuries combined. That is staggering, and undeniable. We consume without considering the consequences of that consumption, often leaving mounds of rubbish in our wake. Yet, if we were to observe the Earth Herself, we would recognize that equilibrium has always been an essential factor in the continuation of Life here on Earth.

Certainly, not all of the natural disasters that have occurred throughout time have humanity as their primary trigger, but the incidents of our contributions to these events have steadily increased with the industrial age. How long can we afford to ignore the natural order of balance? Not long, as many learned people know.

Perhaps it is time to reevaluate the meaning of balance in our minds. Balance does not mean denial, nor does it mean that we will be deprived of what we need to sustain Life. Rather, it means that we have to give as much as we take, and through that effort we could be richly rewarded with the gifts that Nature provides.

There is a twin-ness, a duality that can be observed all around us, beginning with ourselves. The male and female human species was never created to be against one another, but rather to work to bring about our individual strengths so that together we can create a unified whole. The patriarchal systems have not served half of humankind very well, and that single fact alone has given rise to untold hardship and unnecessary mistrust. When any person attempts to dominate another, all balance is lost.

The systems that have separated humanity from itself will not be

201

able to stand forever, and any state of imbalance must be brought back to equilibrium so that all people may thrive. When we are wise enough to hold one another in higher regard, we may just begin to behave in ways worthy of that esteem.

you stand
within a sacred circle
a blessed place
that is you

a place
that holds
your widsom,
your knowledge,
your love
and
your heart

bless others
by inviting
them into
your circle

Elaine M. Grohman

203

THE POWER OF NATURE

*"Nature is an infinite sphere
whose center is everywhere
and whose circumference
is nowhere."*

Blaise Pascal

Spirit Message
May 20, 2011

"Within the torrent of a spring storm, you can see and feel tremendous power. There is power that shakes the trees, bringing downpours of rain, wind and thunder to rattle your windows. This power can bring you to a place of knowing that there is a greater Power beyond yourself.

This Power, the Power of Nature, is Creation's gift to you, to Mother Earth and to all of Her inhabitants. The Power of Nature can bring calm to your heart, wonder to your mind and beauty to your eyes. In all of its wonderment, majesty and beauty, humanity often misses the most important gift that Nature provides. This is the gift of Healing and support.

When your heart is troubled, do not try to find the answers within yourself. Step out into the wonder and magic of Nature and ask

Her to share Her wisdom with you.

That simple, humble act opens the doors of possibility for you to gain insight, peace and solutions to the problems facing you. Nature is designed for balance.

The human being is the only species on Earth that takes years for maturity to occur. Other beings stand firmly on the ground within a matter of minutes, and are able to join with its fellow beings as a welcomed member. It would be wise for humanity to observe Nature's reliance on Nature itself when balance is sought.

As you find yourselves in situations that bring you concern, pause and enter into conversation with Nature. She will surprise and delight you in many beautiful and wondrous ways."

Do you know that Nature can speak to you? People have known it for centuries, trusting that Nature will guide us in every way if we are wise enough to listen. Gardeners know this, and I would bet that most farmers know it too. You ought to try it sometime. Go ahead, talk to Nature when no one else is watching, if you fear being seen.

I attended a gathering about the Teachings of the Ancient Medicine Wheels. We were encouraged to spend time with the Trees and to ask for assistance with finding answers to questions deep within our hearts.

I greeted the sweet, Shaggy Bark Tree that I had attempted to converse with in the past few days and rested my right hand on its trunk, being mindful not to crush the bowed bark of its skin. It felt awkward, as if I was forcing a shy individual to speak to me. Gently my fingertips touched the green moss that clung to its home above the ground. Ever so softly she silently whispered, "Go now to Twin Oak, that you may receive its message to bring back to the Circle of People inside." I felt a slight shock, knowing that my mind was not playing tricks on me.

Walking toward Twin Oak I hesitated for a moment, not wanting to disturb a man sitting on the bench below the massive tree.

"Keep coming," I heard, as I caught a glimpse of a larger bench, surrounded and supported by ancient stones on three sides.

"Look up," Twin Oak said, "you are still under my canopy." I looked to see the youngest branches dancing over my head.

Sitting down, I rested my back against the cool stones. Feeling tucked away and protected, I turned slightly to see the man crying and I asked that Spirit bless his needs and heart.

A small carpet of green moss invited my touch as I nestled against the damp stones. Looking closely, the vibrant green held a tiny droplet of moisture, like a tear shed by the moss as it waited to fall.

I sat and watched a winged friend soar over the valley below, inviting me to rest and watch as he silently glided with the Wind. I marveled at its effortless movement, such steady understanding of the minute movements that would allow his flight to appear smooth and graceful.

"Welcome," Twin Oak said through the tremble of my body.

"Look to your right side and pick up the branch that rests beside you. It holds a message for the Circle of Humans inside."

I listened and picked up the branch from the bench and I brushed a raindrop with my fingers. It disappeared into the fabric of my jeans.

"Look closely now and tell me of the message that awaits you," Twin Oak said. Gently holding the branch I noticed that the stem had four leaves on the right and five leaves on the left. The center was strong and sturdy, allowing Life to come to all of the Leaves through its steady core. There were a total of nine leaves supported by a central branch. Nine plus one equals ten. A complete Circle in the lesson we were learning.

At the top of the branch were five perfectly formed buds - the number that represents Humanity.

Twin Oak stated clearly in my mind, "This is the first complete Circle, the full Ten and Zero. Bring it to the People inside." I was amazed that my answer was presented to me in such a clear and gentle way.

Looking closely, I studied the Gift I held in my hand. I had asked a question and the Tree replied. Twin Oak had gifted me with a tangible gift, as I held a portion of Her Life in my hands. As leaves fall from the trees, we would be wise to think of them as something other than a chore to rake. They have given us the gift of shade during hot summer days. They have given us the melody of the wind through their branches. They have dropped their Life to the ground so that we might enjoy the sound of crushing leaves beneath our feet. They have provided endless hours of fun for children as they jump and play in the discarded leaves that await collection.

A full Circle, a Sacred Zero walked with me into our Ceremony, our Human Circle, our Temple of Wisdom that had so lovingly been shared with us. "The Zero is the symbol and fact of Creation. The Zero Chiefs say that the Zero is not nothing, but is Everything,"(5) as explained by the great Zero Chief Estcheemah, mentor to the author and Medicine Man, Hyemeyohsts Storm, and his wife Swan, my trusted Teachers.

Nature's way is the ultimate lesson: the Wisest Teacher, the Compassionate Mother, the Strong Father, the Willful Brother, the Shy Sister and the Tender Lover. All of it is here for all of us. If only we would ask.

Watch Nature and you will begin to understand balance. Balance is what we need, balance is what we crave.

---

(5) From page 194 of "Lightningbolt" by Hyemeyohsts Storm

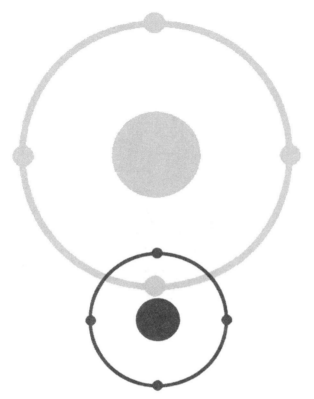

you are always
connected to life
for it surrounds and
supports you
always
and in all ways

Elaine M. Grohman

ELAINE M. GROHMAN

Truth

truth
stands on
solid ground

asking us all
to look within
ourselves

to see
where
truth
lives

Elaine M Grohman

SEEK TRUTH

"Truth has no special time of its own.
Its hour is now - always."

Albert Schweitzer

Spirit Message
June 13, 2011
3:59 pm

"Seek Truth. It is imperative that humanity begins to seek Truth.
Many people speak thoughtlessly, without the clarity needed to
comprehend the impact of their words. Spoken words are like
weapons when used carelessly. Begin to seek Truth and your lives
will change for the better.

In situations where people are exposed to many kinds of people,
such as yourselves, it is easy to make judgments. We stress to
you, do not judge, rather seek to understand.

If you must, make observations about what can be done to help
one another, whether that is with your assistance, your guidance
or your kindness. Do not jump to conclusions, for we tell you
that it is very easy to misunderstand the real events that are taking
place.

With open and loving hearts, seek Truth, and then be willing to guide others with loving examples. If unkindness is being spoken, stop it in its tracks. If judgment is being heard, ask, "is what you believe the truth?"

Then bring Peace to your world with open and loving lives. We ask this of you and we pray that you will listen. Begin today, begin now."

Our world is changing at a rapid pace. Events are accelerating that are bringing about a global consciousness, whether we like it or not. Across the planet, citizenry are peacefully taking a stand against dictators, corruption, and inequality and are standing up for basic human dignity. Balance is needed and balance will be found. Humanity is seeking what Mother Earth is seeking – equilibrium.

Balance requires change - and change is inevitable. Before true balance can be attained, however, we must scrupulously examine everything. We are in need of a whole new way of thinking, a whole new way of conceptualizing, a whole new way of imagining, so that wholesome changes can be brought about swiftly and efficiently, all the while taking the whole of humanity into consideration.

The human imagination has produced amazing things and is doing so all of the time. It is time for capitalists to change what they capitalize upon – financial gain or Life itself. This change requires Truth, Integrity and Open Disclosure, virtues that have often been silenced in most forms of governance.

We must allow for continual cross-examination of our individual thinking and the ways in which we manage ourselves. From our households to the grander scale of our global responsibility, the call for Balance is being heard. Before change can occur, we must evaluate how things have been done in the past in order to reverse the destructive behaviors we have permitted to become our norm.

Constructive change requires examination of what is, so that our minds can become fertile ground for new concepts to be envisioned, allowing us to see the possibility of how things should and could be done. Balance brings about freedom from involuntary servitude for all people, on all continents, in all cities and villages and in all households. If there is inequality anywhere we can no longer afford to ignore it.

Escalating health care costs, escalating unemployment and countless other stressors are forcing us to look at life differently. Things are not working, and we all know it.

I happened to walk by two colleagues, both gifted healers, who were discussing the parallel situations that they were encountering daily in their separate workplaces – difficult bosses. The elegant woman was describing her superior as a woman who frequently reprimanded her for being "too nice," while the gentleman was vexed by his boss who was continually attempting to push people's buttons, with the intent of causing an argument. Certainly neither of these situations is conducive to a healthy nor productive working environment.

Poorly managed leadership is not leadership at all. It is a condoned abuse of power.

The two healers had been attempting to withstand the barrage of insults and insinuations by trying to "energetically protect" themselves, but to no avail. I stood and listened quietly and then asked if I might make a suggestion. "What if you were to consider saying to that individual, 'How does it help you to behave in this way?' literally bringing the problems that they are causing squarely into their own laps, where they belong," I said.

We have allowed the bully on the block to become the bully in the boardroom. And the truth is, anyone who bullies another possesses neither self-leadership nor self-responsibility and are ill equipped to lead others. Any corporation or office that allows bullying to continue has doomed itself to failure.

There are problems in our workplaces and they can be seen in almost every institution and industry, and the problem is that people have lost their sense of dignity and decorum, allowing their own insecurities and unkindness to be spewed upon those with whom they work, as if it were their alienable right to do so. We have an opportunity to rethink our positions in the workplace and in the world. We ought to become our own CEO's – Chief Energy Operators – the one who has possession and exclusive sovereign right to our dignity and self-regard.

For far too long we have been willing to withstand abuse. Abuse in the workplace, abuse in the schools, abuse in the home and abuse in our own minds. It is time to correct our thinking and our behavior and begin to conduct ourselves as civilized men and women. The abuse of authority can corrupt our thinking and our hearts. Inevitably, left unchecked, the undisciplined ruler can become a dictator in no time. Once a dictatorship has begun, all balance is lost. Whether that is in a county, a company or a household, everyone will eventually lose.

To ignore the ranting of a bully is foolish. If allowed to continue, it will be fatal to any relationship. And let's face it; all commerce is based upon relationships. If relationships erode, then the integrity of the company will eventually follow. It is time to look differently at our relationships with one another and begin to see other humans as potential allies rather than as potential enemies. It is better to end a battle before it begins by stopping it in its tracks, taking away the need to defend, and stopping the unending blustering of egos that have run amuck.

Turning the tide of responsibility to rest squarely in the lap of the abuser, we can relinquish our fear of standing up to presumed authority and, as in the children's tale, tell the emperor that he has no cloths on. To complain about abuse does nothing to change it, but challenging it just might.

Our imbalances are self-imposed and therefore balance can be self-initiated. Systemic changes in one system can bring about systemic changes in another. Let's begin. Together.

the way you view
your life
influences the way
you view
your world

Elaine M. Grohman

216

YOUR HOME - MOTHER EARTH

"As for the Future,
your task is not to foresee
but to enable it."

Antoine de Saint-Exupery

Spirit Message
June 23, 2011
5:20 pm

"Dearest Ones, the Earth is not only your home, She is your greatest gift, for without her, your life would not be possible. It is our fervent hope that you would begin to appreciate Mother Earth and the multitude of gifts she provides. For far too long, the gifts that she has provided have been seen as replaceable, unimportant and disposable. Nothing could be further from the Truth. All that is provided for you.... the air that you breath, the food that you eat, the beauty around you, the nature that brings you comfort, the water that quenches your thirst and cleanses your body...all of this and more, comes from Mother Earth. She needs you to care for her, and she needs you to care for yourselves.

As humanity begins to appreciate Mother Earth, it is our greatest hope that you will begin to respect, honor and love yourselves as well. The thoughts of humanity bring about more destruction than the most violent hurricane or the swiftest tsunami. Your self talk can be likened to the most dangerous poison or the most bountiful harvest. It all depends upon you.

We ask that you no longer compartmentalize your lives, falsely believing the illusion of separation, one from another. You are intimately connected to all things, all creatures, all of nature and all of humanity. Be mindful, now and always, of the impact of your thoughts, your words, your deeds and your silence. All thoughts, actions, words and deeds are known throughout Creation, and this you must know. No longer pretend that your thoughts don't matter, no longer pretend that your words don't matter, no longer pretend that your actions don't matter, for it all matters.

Be your best selves from this day forward, and you will truly love your neighbor as yourself. And when you love your neighbor and yourselves, you will love this Earth and all that inhabit her. The seen and the unseen need your blessings and attention. And in that you will bring Peace to your hearts, health to your bodies, and balance to the world in which you live. Do not delay for every moment not lived with a loving and joyful heart is a moment lost to the beauty and treasure of knowing your truest selves. Bless yourselves, bless your neighbor and bless Mother Earth. Then Live Consciously."

I felt numb, with an interesting mixture of awe, wonder and a tinge of hyper-alertness. My aunt was a hospice patient, dying in her own home from the end stages of diabetes. As she lay motionless in a coma-like state, I held her near lifeless hand and thanked her for all that she had done for us. She momentarily opened her eyes to tell me that she could see her sister. "Then you go to her darlin', because she will take good care of you," I said.

The sister that she could so clearly see was my own precious mother who had died twenty-seven years before, when I was just thirteen years old. In the blink of an eye she slipped back into a coma-like state. In that instant there was a palpable movement in the air, an unseen force that to this day brings shivers down my spine. I had hoped my mother would be there to greet his younger sister, and my hopes were confirmed in that moment.

This event propelled me into a whole new world and provided an intimate look at the dynamic energy of the Human Spirit and our intimate connection with all that surrounds us. In short order I became a hospice volunteer, a student of Energy Medicine and a new person. All that I had suspected about our connection to the Divine was corroborated in seemingly mysterious ways that further opened my intuition.

As an avid gardener, I had realized the tremendous benefits of working in the soil. Many times I would find myself working through concerns as I carefully tilled the soil and often found myself in deep conversations with Creation. I had a million questions and if I were quiet I would receive guidance as I knelt to work the dirt. A garden needs tending, and so does our Lives. A healthy garden begins with a healthy foundation.

It seemed natural for me to recognize the deep connection between Nature and Humanity, and I had an idea. I wondered if the
hospice facility would be interested in expanding the existing garden space adjacent to the building. I envisioned a private garden
that patients and families could enjoy in order to have a momentary respite from the inevitable difficulty of saying good-bye to
the physical world.

I knew the comfort that Nature brought me, and it was my hope
to bring that same peace to whoever might be in need. Sitting in
the staff office of the hospice facility I asked the volunteer manager and the director if I could have permission to proceed with
creating a garden. "How will you find the time, money and people?" they asked. "Leave it to me," I assured them.

I set to work with a plan in mind. I have a group of friends who
themselves are avid gardeners, and an opportunity presented itself
to ask for their assistance with creating a hospice garden. I shared
my thoughts and they all readily agreed. My intention was to engage the community in the project, with the hope of helping others understand that dying is a part of living, and with that
recognition, perhaps, just perhaps, we all would begin to live our
lives differently.

Before long the garden was designed, the soil was tilled, the
plants were delivered and planted, and all that we had hoped for
had come to fruition. A gazebo, fountain, sculpture and pergola
enhanced the beauty of the garden. Creation was supporting the
project in remarkable ways and in no time the dedication day had
arrived. Through the efforts of dozens of people a magnificent
garden flourished. Shortly after the dedication, I received a letter
of thanks that made all of the work worthwhile.

The garden was designed in a large circle, with private seating areas encircling the garden. The pathway was wide enough that a hospital bed could easily be maneuvered through the garden, allowing patients to soak in the sunshine and fragrances in privacy. The rhythmic sound of falling water as it splashed on the rocks below drowned out the sounds of tears that needed to fall.

It was a beautifully sunny day and one of the patients requested her family bring her outside. Her daughter lovingly wheeled her around the garden, describing the rich colors and textures that her mother's eyes could no longer see. Grandchildren picked flowers and decorated their grandmother's bed and laughed and played while mother and daughter spent precious time together. It was her final day, and sometime during the night she quietly slipped away from her failing body.

Her daughter sent me a letter thanking me for the efforts of all of those who worked to bring the garden to a reality. She wrote, "Thank you for helping to make my mother's last day so beautiful." My heart swelled with gratitude for all of the people who toiled to make the garden the sanctuary that it was. It was exactly as I envisioned it – a magical place where the beauty of Nature could be appreciated – even on a grandma's last day.

CHANGE, CHANGE, CHANGE

"You cannot step twice
into the same river;
for other waters
are always flowing on to you."
Heraclitus

Spirit Message
June 27, 2011
5:31 pm

"What do you want your day to be? Indeed, what do you want
your life to be? Have you thought of the importance of those
questions? What do you want? Do you even know?

Many of your hours and days are spent in busyness. Are you
spending as much of your time as you would like in making sure
that your busyness is meaningful? This does not mean that you
should dismiss everyday activities as if they were unimportant.
No, rather, make everything you do important to you, and you
will find your mind and your heart will change.

Begin to take care of everything that you do, and that care will
change you. It is time for you to think about all that you do so
that you might change your thinking. Change your thinking and

change your life. Change your mind and change your life. Change your heart and change your life.

It is time to dismiss the notion that things must be difficult, tiresome, drudgery or simply something other than what you would like to be doing. If you changed your perspective and began to appreciate all that you do, think and say, your whole perspective would change.

This is an important time to embrace the opportunity of change. Change for the better is simply a thought away. Change your mind, change your life. Change your heart, change the world."

During the time of the hospice garden's construction, other opportunities began to blossom, when I was offered a position on the staff as a full time employee. This enabled me to become more fully integrated into the hospice organization and created opportunities for me to developing my organizational, writing and speaking skills. While working at hospice I was simultaneously enrolled in a course of study called Polarity Therapy, a form of Energy Medicine. I continued to work there for a year and a half.

But before long, my time at hospice was coming to an end. I felt that I had accomplished all that I could and I was ready to begin my life as an energy healer. I knew that I was taking an enormous leap of faith and I was ready for that leap.

My last day at the hospice organization was full of farewells and good wishes. As I sat in my office in the corporate headquarters I silently asked that my last day be used for the benefit of another.

Within a few minutes the telephone rang. The social worker was on the line asking if I might be able to find a volunteer to sit with a gentleman that I had met the day before. It was clear that he was failing and he did not want to die alone.

His family was having a difficult time with his impending death and he did not want to add to their strain by asking them to be present. His wife was caring for an ill daughter and out of love for both of them he thought it best that they stay home.

It was getting late in the afternoon, and I realized that my request had been granted. I told her that I would come to sit with him; after all, it was too late to contact a volunteer. Just the day before as I walked down the hall of the facility towards the staff office, I was stopped by a woman asking me to come into a patient's room to be a witness for him as he signed his will. It was the same man. When I met the gentleman, his soft eyes showed his gentle nature, and he quietly thanked me for my time. I told him that I was happy to help him.

Curiously, later that same evening I felt the need to stop at a local gift store, although I really wasn't sure why. There was beautiful harp music playing on the store's sound system and I stood transfixed by the sound. Inquiring if this music was for sale, the clerk smiled and handed me the CD. "I love this music, don't you?" she asked. I did love the music. I had known that music therapists in both hospice and palliative care settings often used harp music. The soft, gentle sound of the melodic harp would often induce a deep sense of relaxation, allowing muscle tension and fears to fade away. This relaxation would provide an opening for release from an ailing body.

Driving to the hospice facility to be with the gentleman that last day, I noticed that I still had the harp music CD on the seat beside me. Pulling into the parking lot I decided to bring it in with me. His room had a soft glow from the afternoon sun and the autumn colors of the trees outside made the windows look like jeweled stained glass. I asked if he would like to hear some soft music. "That would be wonderful," he said in a whisper. I placed the CD in the player and the room filled with the magical, melodic sound of the harp.

His room faced the garden and he was gazing outside as I entered his private sanctuary. "Thank you for coming," he said quietly. "It is my honor to be here," I replied. We talked about the garden outside and he told me how grateful he was to have such a beautiful view.

Sitting by his left side he asked if I would mind holding his hand. I gently placed his fragile hands in mine, marveling at the contrast of his thin skin against my own healthy one. His grip was solid and I imagined all the many things he must have done with his hands throughout his life. He had a sweet smile that seemed to make his face glow with an inner knowing of his journey yet to come.

Every now and then he raised our joined hands to his mouth and gently kissed my hand, saying over and over, "Thank you for being here with me." Tears rolled down my cheeks as I smiled. He began to drift in and out of sleep, and each time he awoke he kissed my hand again and smiled. No words needed to be said.

After awhile the physician came into the room to see if he was comfortable. Standing across from me, the gentleman reached for the physician's hand and held it within his own. For a moment, he looked back and forth between the doctor and I, smiling all the while and then softly said, "I think you both know what this is all about, don't you?" We both nodded our heads in agreement.

The nurse came into the room and the gentleman told her that he had reconsidered and that he wanted to have his wife and daughter with him as he took his last breath. He asked if she would call and ask them to come. I was happy for them, and waited until they arrived before I would take my leave. Before I left he said these words to me. "Thank you for being with me. I now know that it is important that my family be with me too. I hope that God blesses you in all that you do." I thanked him and tears fell from my eyes as his family entered the room.

There is sacredness during the dying process that allows us to witness the beauty of a human life. I was grateful to be a momentary visitor in the final hours of this gentleman's journey here on Earth. I knew that my time at hospice was complete. Now it was time to help people in a different way. It was my hope that through Energy Healing I might be able to assist others in releasing their wounds so that their lives could be full of greater possibilities.

THE SOURCE
OF LASTING PEACE

"There are only two ways to live your life.
One is as though nothing is a miracle.
The other is as though
everything is a miracle."

Albert Einstein

Spirit Message
June 29, 2011
2:52 pm

"Now is the time for hearts to be still and to listen. You have heard the fearful cries of those who choose to control others with their illusions of power. Control is employed by the fearful and ultimately they will lose the illusory power that they so desperately cling to.

Now is the time for Self-Responsibility and Self-Leadership, which examines and employs the best of the self and brings that goodness forward for the betterment of Humanity. The illusion of power is losing its power, for the real and lasting power is within the Human Heart. All the forms of illusory power that have attempted to control humanity are losing ground, and that loss is igniting their fear and ultimately their hostility.

You have seen it unfold around you. Within your homes, within your relationships, within your workplace, there is no place in which false power has not attempted to gain ground. That ground has no foundation as it is like quicksand that will devour the one who seeks to struggle for control of others. To attempt to control another is an act of violence, and Love has no place within it.

Do not react, for that reaction will often be equally hostile. Rather, quiet yourself and seek to engage the Divine Love and Light that is within you. Be still and bring the Power of Love forward so that the fear that drives false power can be seen for what it is... the Omission of Love from Human interactions. Nothing can flourish without Love as its guiding force. Nothing will fall harder than control that has no love. Love commands, it does not control.

Look around you and witness the fall of those whose power has brought nothing but heartache, injury and a whole host of atrocities, in a desperate attempt to maintain power at all costs.

Whether it is happening in countries, corporations, institutions or families, it is time for humanity to come to grips with the problems inherent in the illusion of power so that real Power may finally be employed.

True and lasting Power is the hallmark of Love. Love brings balance, care, integrity and wholeness to all that it encounters, and allows humanity to bring forward the best of itself. Throughout history, man has grasped power and lost its heart. There will never be peace in those circumstances.

Now it is time to bless those whose distress is destructive, for ultimately they destroy themselves first and will have to answer to every thought, word and action that they undertake. Look care-fully, dear Ones, and be cautious with your reactions so as not to feed the fire of fear that resides in those who are willing to attempt to manipulate others.

The Power of Love can move mountains, dissolve hatred, banish fear and open the heart to the possibility of inclusion of new ideas and ways of being.

You may need to walk away from those things that bring harm, as you feel the rumble of its crumbling foundation. Do not let that bring you fear. It is time to re-invent yourselves, to bring the Authority of Love that is your Birthright, indeed of what you are made. Love is the foundation of anything lasting and real. Love respects, Love guides, Love listens, Love is open to many points of view and Love ultimately is the Cause of all Goodness, and the Source of Lasting Peace."

I am constantly amazed by the way things happen in my life. Seemingly out of the blue, a book that I need is recommended, or someone who knows some information that I am trying to find crosses my path. It happens all of the time. But it never happens by accident. I know better. Nothing happens by accident.

Just as certainly, our healings do not happen by accident either. To heal any situation we must bring our attention to the problem. Ignoring a problem has never solved anything. Action taken in the direction of correction, however, has great Power inherent within that action.

These experiences teach me, time and again, that life is not random, and that we can have far more influence in our lives than we might have previously believed. When we begin to step into our own Power, the Power to use our Hearts and our Minds for the benefit of others, the Universe will support those efforts in the most surprising of ways.

The late Ceremonial Chief and Medicine Man of the Teton Sioux, Fool's Crow,(6) spoke these words, *"Survival of the world depends on our sharing what we have, and working together. If we don't the whole world will die. First the planet, and next the people."* He continued by saying, *"The ones who complain and talk the most about giving away Medicine Secrets are always those who know the least."*

Fools' Crow warned that anyone who attempted to keep blessings to themselves had no real power, they merely attempted to abuse the weak power that they perceived themselves to have. True Power is a Gift and a Responsibility. And it was understood, by all Native Peoples, that any abuse of power would lead to the absolute stripping of power from that individual. Without respect for Power, Humanity would be forever at the mercy of madmen - power hungry individuals who seek to control others while having no true self control themselves.

We as a Human Race are in the midst of our greatest challenges as well as our greatest opportunities. Stepping away from illusory power helps all of us look deep within ourselves to see our own Humanity. Those individuals whose position, rank or title may inflate their egos will soon find that their careers are over and they are stuck with the problems that they have created.

Resist the temptation to blame and ridicule, which can be very counterproductive. Be an observer rather than a judge, and you will begin to break down barriers that are held in place by your perceptions. Regardless of social status or political rank, we all want the same things. We want Love, we want Prosperity, and we want Peace. If that is your truth, then work for it. Start with Yourself.

(6) To learn more about Fool's Crow, please see the website below as well as other books about his life.

http://www.spiritual-endeavors.org/native/frank.htm

the beauty
that surrounds
you
is also
within
you

Elaine M. Grohman

YOU ARE FREE TO JUDGE...
OR NOT

*"Real generosity toward the future
lies in giving all to the present."*

Albert Camus

Spirit Message
July 28, 2011
7:57 am

*"Release. Release. Release. Release yourselves from the chains
that bind you. Within each individual is the potential for imprisonment. It happens every day, throughout your day, as you im-
prison yourselves with judgment, limiting thoughts and anger.
Release yourselves from this imprisonment and Live freely.*

*Each and every moment, you are free to judge - or not. You are
free to complain - or not. You are free to be angry - or not. Which
do you choose? Each choice can be a new beginning, a new and
fresh way of looking at your life, those around you and Mother
Earth. You do not see or even appreciate most of the things that
you are doing.*

In daily life you do things without thinking. You eat without think-

ing. You react without thinking and you withhold without think-
ing. We ask you to become Conscious of Everything that you do
so that Life can begin to open in new and wondrous ways for you.
Put aside the destructive rhetoric with which you speak to your-
selves and others.

When was the last time you thought about and then appreciated
the land upon which you live? When was the last time you
thought about and then appreciated the food that you eat? This
life that sustains your life is a Gift to you. It is not something to
be done blindly but rather appreciated, so that your food can be-
come your medicine, your Good Medicine that can reduce or re-
lieve your body's pain. The miracle that takes place in your own
physiology each and every second is rarely contemplated by hu-
manity, until there is failure of the system.

Do not fail yourselves dear Friends. Gift yourselves with aware-
ness and Love. Appreciation will change everything."

A client came to me concerned about her stress. It was taking its
toll on her life. Her health, her sleeping and her emotions were
all over the map. She admitted that the least little provocation
would set her off. She would immediately react and stay angry
for hours, sometimes days. She was distressed by her seeming
lack of control.

When she asked what I thought the problem might be I suggested
two probable causes. First, perhaps she was unwilling to relinquish her anger about the past. As a result, when similar stressors
presented themselves she would react in a habitual manner – with

anger and resentment. There was a simple enough solution, I assured her. Perhaps she would be willing to forgive the past so that she could look at things differently. At first she seemed a bit disturbed by this notion, but fairly quickly she realized that she had not forgiven the past at all.

Forgiveness does not release another from the responsibility for any wrong doing, but rather allows you to relinquish your need to react, and more likely, over react, with energy robbing emotions such as anger, fear and resentment. When we neglect to forgive the past, we fall into the repetitive patterns of anger, fear, and frustration that, left unchecked, will eventually become draining. The entire body reacts to stress – body, mind, Spirit and emotions and habitual responses can be a precursor to stress and ultimately illness.

When forgiveness is given, we give ourselves the gift of awareness – an often-overlooked component of forgiveness. Many times, people are angry about incidences that took place years ago, and the offender may not even be aware that there was a problem to begin with. Anger held within causes damage within. It is a fact and a tragedy that years may be wasted when we are unwilling to relinquish anger.

When forgiveness is needed, remind yourself of what you may have learned about yourself in the process. You may just be surprised. You might learn that you are resilient, that you are thoughtful, that you are cognizant of your words; you may have learned that you are more than what others think or say about you. The opportunity for self-examination can be very revealing.

The second, and in my mind, the more important action that she could take was to become grounded. Being grounded is physical and the sensations of being grounded are palpable – physically, emotionally and spiritually. There are simple techniques that assist in helping energy to move effectively through the human body that, in turn, raises the frequency of the body and we begin to calm down. When energy is low, we often feel ill equipped to handle normal everyday stress. Couple that with the demands of busy careers, money concerns, rising costs, and the world situation, it is easy to see how people might escalate out of control, all of which is neither productive or conducive to clear thinking and even emotions.

Let's change our unhealthy patterns of behavior and thinking that has caused us such unnecessary distress. It is up to each and every one of us.

THE TRUE ACT OF COMMUNION

*"A wise man's heart
guides his mouth."*

Proverbs 16:23

Spirit Message
August 18, 2011
11:44 am

"Be willing to speak your mind, but remember to use your Heart. There is too much incomplete communication that prevents clear understanding. There is always an opportunity to speak your mind. Speaking your mind can be an enormous gift for yourself and others. Speaking your mind while engaging your heart will open doors of understanding.

So often people miss the opportunity for full communion with others. Communion is defined as the act of sharing, and should be done with the intention of clear communication. Being open, honest and sharing of one's feelings and ideas eliminates unnecessary hardships that half-truths can create.

We ask that you consider the importance of the act of communion - the act of sharing.

But first, it is important to recognize what you wish to communicate. Be clear in your own understanding if any hard feelings or misunderstanding are in play. Bring clarity to your words so that the barriers of mistrust can fall away.

Let Love be the reason you speak, so that the Love that You are can be known."

The human ability to communicate is one of our greatest gifts. We are free to express ourselves in a multitude of ways through sight, touch and sound. We express ourselves through the written word, through music, through movement and with our voices. We have the ability to convey the depths of our emotions, often, without uttering a word. Our actions, our facial expressions and our body language can communicate emotions when words fail us. The human eyes are truly "the windows of the soul" and can explicitly convey the depths of our feelings of rage, anger, mistrust, compassion, joy, laughter and love. The entire gamut of emotions transmits our thinking and our hearts in a matter of seconds.

Now is the perfect time for all of us to contemplate the importance of this incredible gift – our gift of communication. Now is the perfect time to evaluate how effectively we communicate our thoughts and feelings so that we might set into motion clear understanding of our wants, needs and desires. Now is the time to carefully evaluate what we wish to convey about our world concerns and ourselves so that unnecessary discord can be halted before it can even begin.

We don't need to look far to see the suffering and hardship that our veiled communications have created. Begin this day to think before you speak, to listen to your own heart so that problems and misunderstandings can be prevented or resolved more swiftly. Speak your words with clear and unwavering Truth, with the Love that is within You as the Guiding presence of Goodness and Peace, that there will be no room for misunderstanding. Relinquish resentment, for its damage can be long lasting. And, if resolution is not possible, give yourself the space to consider other options, other points of view and other potential solutions.

This is our World, our Home and our Planet – Mother Earth. We must care for Her as She has cared for us. We must honor the multitude of life forms that inhabit this Earth along with us, so that all may flourish. Every species has a right to be here. Every Human Being has the right to be here. Let us begin to teach one another through Love, so that Love will be the Force that guides us so that our Spirits will Awaken.

Acknowledgments

*"To be Born
is our most precious gift.
No other Truth is so dear."*

Estcheemah

Our lives are extraordinary and singularly unique. No other person in the whole of humanity has had identical experiences, thoughts, emotions or interpretations as us. This can be both a challenge and a wonderful opportunity for expansions and growth as individuals and as a species. Our diversity is our blessing.

For me, I am eternally grateful for those individuals that I have been blessed to have in my Life. Each person is unique – I treasure the endless opportunities these people have provided me to grow as a woman, as a healer, as a wife, as a sister, as a mother, as a grandmother, as a teacher and as a friend. It is through our experiences with one another that we develop and grow into the multi-faceted individuals Creation intended for us to be. It is the very purpose of our Lives.

I would like to thank some of the people who have helped to bring this book to print. My daughter, Lainie Rubio, who has been my steadfast assistant on this journey, for helping to organize my schedule so I was free to write, teach and help others. In that process, she gained an awareness of her own profoundly moving gifts. And to her wonderful husband, Marvin, who beautifully co-parents our grandchildren, Maria, Conner and Isabella as they blossom into the amazing people that they are.

To my son Brian and his beautiful wife Ronya. Through mutual respect and love they have grown together, always including family and friends in the process as their life together unfolds and expands with the love that they share. For Brian, whose work ethic and integrity are his calling cards and will serve him and his family well in the coming years. I am a proud Mama.

For my husband, Rich, who has worked for years through incredible pain and who has learned to open his own heart in the process. I am grateful for all that you have done and continue to do for me.

For my many brothers and sisters, nieces and nephews, and all my friends, relatives and Teachers, I would not be the person that I am without you in my Life.

For my friends, Kelly D'Souza and Tracy Kroll, for your generosity and scrutiny in reviewing the text of this manuscript so that my words are clean and my punctuation improved. Thank you for your time and constructive evaluation. A big thank you to my friend, Laurie Tennent for her beautiful photography and masterful eye. I am grateful to all of you for your friendship.

And for all of you whose stories have touched my Life, continually illustrating in real and concrete fashion, how Spirit talks to all of us, in both big and small ways. The message is always the same. The Message is Love.

With gratitude,
Elaine

FOOTNOTES & REFERENCES

FOOTNOTES

Chapter 1: Taken from History Confidential – Morsels of Little Known History Facts

http://www.historyconfidential.com/2009/06/the-origin-of-wall-street

Chapters 8 and 41: Hyemeyohsts Storm – http://www.hyemeyohstsstorm.com

Author of *"Seven Arrows"*, *"Lightningbolt"* and *"Song of Heyoehkah"*

Chapter 10: To learn more about LuLu Life please see:

http://www.lulu-life.ch/?sLang=en

LuLu Life documentary -

"The Brillance of Oil" produced by InFocus Productions,

Chapter 30: To learn more about the nuraghi, see the following website:

http://ac-support.europe.umuc.edu/~jmatthew/naples/nuraghipage.htm

Chapter 31: To learn more about the Blanket Bogs of Ireland, see the following website:

http://www.wesleyjohnston.com/users/ireland/geography/bogs.html

Chapter 45: To learn more about Fool's Crow, see website below.

http://www.spiritual-endeavors.org/native/frank.htm

REFERENCES

Cover photo: by Laurie Tennent Laurie Tennent Studio – Birmingham, Michigan

www.laurietennentstudio.com

Crop Circle images: courtesy of Freddy Silva.

www.cropcirclesecrets.org

Hyemeyohsts Storm's schedule please see:

www.circlesofwisdom.wordpress.com

National Hospice and Palliative Care Organization

http://www.nhpco.org

Elaine M. Grohman
www.elainegrohman.com

step forward
confidently
let your strength
be in knowing
that you follow
an unseen path

Elaine M. Grohman

ABOUT THE AUTHOR

*Elaine M. Grohman is a Certified Healing Touch Practitioner, an Associate Polarity Practitioner, an Angel Therapy Practitioner, and the developer and teacher of an energy healing modality called **Sacred Geometry and Energy Medicine – Healing from the Fourth Dimension, Levels I and II**. She has an active private practice in which she sees clients for both Energy Healing and Angel Readings. As an Angel Reader, she conducts Audience Angel Readings, giving messages of love and comfort to as many people as possible.*

Along with her private practice, Elaine is involved with the University of Michigan Medical School's Integrative Medicine Program. She enjoys working with medical students, residents, Integrative Medicine Fellows, physicians, and medical faculty to help them understand Energy Medicine, Integrative Medicine and its place in health care. She also works with medical students from Wayne State University Medical School in Detroit, Michigan and their HuMed program for first year medical students. She is a guest lecturer at Madonna University in Livonia, Michigan in both their nursing and hospice programs.

She is the former host of "Going Beyond Medicine," on Psychic Radio, owned and operated by CBS. In that capacity, she interviewed experts, authors and individuals who are making a difference in health care through Integrative Medicine. Her guests also included individuals whose expertise helps to support self-growth, health and awareness of Body, Mind, Spirit and Emotions.

Elaine and her husband Rich live in Farmington Hills, Michigan. She is the mother of two wonderful human beings, Elaine Rubio and Brian Grohman. Her family is blessed with their son-in-law, Marvin, and their daughter-in-law Ronya, along with three beautiful grandchildren, Maria, Conner and Isabella. Elaine is also blessed to have fourteen siblings, two of whom are deceased, many in-laws and a whole host of nieces and nephews. Our family continues to grow with each passing year.

*Her first book, **The Angels and Me - Experiences of Receiving and Sharing Divine Communications**, published in 2009, is available through Amazon and other online retailers, as well as from her website. It will soon be released in electronic formats.*

Please look for her third book, as yet untitled, which is due for release in 2012. In it she explores our need for healing and the ways in which healing can be attained.

Elaine teaches workshops and is available to speak to groups interested in understanding Energy Medicine, our connection to Spirit and Mother Earth.

Elaine's third book, due for release in 2012, will delve into Energy Medicine, Integrative Medicine, the changing face of allopathic medicine and the source of our wounds.

Elaine M. Grohman, CHTP, APP, ATP
Farmington Hills, Michigan USA

Email: elaine@elainegrohman.com
Website: www.elainegrohman.com